CHRONICLES OF LITTLE GIDDING

Church of St John the Divine,
Little Gidding

CHRONICLES
OF
LITTLE GIDDING

BY

ALAN MAYCOCK

LONDON

S·P·C·K

1954

*First published in 1954
by S.P.C.K.
Northumberland Avenue, London, W.C.2*

*Printed in Great Britain by
Richard Clay and Company, Ltd., Bungay, Suffolk*

FOR ENID WITH LOVE

ACKNOWLEDGEMENTS

My warm thanks are expressed to the Master and Fellows of Magdalene College, Cambridge, for allowing me, with every freedom, to consult the collection of Ferrar MSS in their possession and to publish the material from that collection that appears in this book. I also thank the Master and Fellows of Clare College for equally generous facilities and for permission to include the transcript of " The Arminian Nunnery ".

CONTENTS

INTRODUCTION

IN recent years the story of Little Gidding has become quite widely known. Many people have read the moving account of the Ferrar household in *John Inglesant*—an account which is in the main very accurate. Several modern books have enriched our knowledge and deepened our understanding of that remarkable family enterprise, a thing quite private and obscure, yet displaying to those who have eyes to see, a pattern of Christian living whose inspiration is vividly felt at the present time. During the last few years many pilgrims have visited Little Gidding. There is not a great deal to be seen there—only the little church with the tomb of Nicholas Ferrar before the west door and the gravestones of other members of his family round about. Yet to every pilgrim to Little Gidding there comes a compelling awareness that this is holy ground from which the sanctity will never depart.

Some few years ago the present writer published a book about Nicholas Ferrar. The narrative ended with Ferrar's death in 1637 and several reviewers were good enough to express the hope that there might be a sequel to carry the story on into the later years. This seemed an enterprise well worth attempting, since nothing of the kind had been done before, and since the Magdalene College manuscripts yielded a good deal of entirely new information, not only about Little Gidding itself, but about the fortunes of the various members of the family after they had dispersed from home. In the pages that follow, the attempt is made to present, in as connected a form as possible, an account, first of the events covered by the twenty years between Nicholas's death in 1637 and the death of John Ferrar in 1657, and then of various episodes and happenings connected with Little Gidding which take us on almost to the middle of the eighteenth century, when the estate passed finally out of the hands of the Ferrars.

It was in 1743 that the Reverend Francis Peck, a country

clergyman in Lincolnshire, completed his definitive biography of Nicholas Ferrar, to which he gave the title *The Complete Church of England Man, exemplified in the holy life of Mr. N. Ferrar.* The manuscript was bequeathed by him to John Ferrar's great grandson, Edward Ferrar of Huntingdon, and in turn inherited, along with the great collection of family papers now at Magdalene, by his son-in-law Dr Peter Peckard, Master of the college. It was lent by Peckard to an eccentric clergyman, the Reverend John Jones, who had been for nine years (from 1741 to 1750) vicar of Alconbury, a few miles from Gidding on the Huntingdon side. What subsequently happened is not known; the manuscript was not returned and has never been seen since. It must now be regarded as a complete loss; and wherever two or three friends of Little Gidding are gathered together, the name of John Jones may with fitness be sulphurously anathematized.

Peck's title was an admirable one. "The Complete Church of England Man" is as fine a description as one could wish of Nicholas Ferrar. An absolute loyalty to the Anglican Church, a devout love of her liturgy and an intrinsic understanding of a tradition that was still tentative and unformed—these were the keynotes of a way of life and worship wrought into a marvellous harmony in that remote country household three hundred years ago. To Nicholas both Popery and Puritanism were "arrant novelties" and the mission of the Church of England was, quite simply, to recover the purity of primitive doctrine and practice. This was the principle that he sought to realize at Little Gidding. Some days before he took to his bed in what was to be his last illness, he was walking with his brother John in the great parlour and he began speaking with deep emotion.

"My dear brother," he said. "I am now shortly to appear before my good Lord God, to Whom I must give account of what I have said and taught you all of this family, in the ways and service of God. I have, I tell you, delivered unto you all nothing but what is agreeable to His holy law, will and word, how you should love Him, serve Him, and have shewed you the right good way that leadeth to life everlasting; what you ought to believe, what to do and practise, according to those abilities as

God shall give each one of you and places He shall call you unto. It is the right, good, old way you are in; keep in it. God will be worshipped in spirit and truth, in soul and in body; He will have both inward love and fear, and outward reverence of body and gesture. You, I say, know the way; keep in it. I will not use more words now; you have lessons enough given you. Be constant to them."

He went on to warn John of the trials and sad times that lay ahead, exhorting him strenuously to be courageous and faithful and to maintain the daily prayers and that " they should stedfastly and constantly adhere to the doctrine of the Church of England ". It was a solemn charge, summarizing all the precepts and guidance that he had given them during the twelve years of their common life at Gidding. During those years the joy and inspiration that they had found in their Anglican heritage had been the greater because in large measure they had been discovering its treasures for themselves. This is an important point. It had not been a matter of following long-established usages: there were none to follow. Rather had they, when they came to Gidding, entered into a tradition whose riches were as yet unexplored and even, in some sense, unsuspected; so that, as the fulness of their way of life was worked out, they found themselves thanking Almighty God for that He had indeed kept the good wine until now.

The Reformation in England had followed a fumbling, opportunist course in which the Church was given little chance of speaking its mind. By the end of Elizabeth's reign the conflict had, for the time being, worked itself out. The Anglican Church, with its state-imposed liturgy and its rigidly regimented membership, was as yet without any conscious tradition and without anything that could be called a coherent theology. The Elizabethan theologians were, for the most part, dull and undistinguished men. The Book of Common Prayer, drawn up in the febrile atmosphere of the mid-century controversies, was still a battleground; and in some respects those who detested it were nearer to a true understanding of its character than those who upheld and used it.

At the turn of the century it might have seemed that the Church of England was destined within a few years to perish of sheer inanition or at best to become an obedient and spiritually negligible department of state. It was at this moment that the first beginnings of a remarkable regeneration became, almost of a sudden, discernible. Theology woke to new life in the writings of Andrewes and Hooker; indeed, the importance of these two men in the history of Anglicanism can hardly be exaggerated. They were in no sense innovators. They were rather restorers, seeking to recover for the Church of England the fulness of the Christian inheritance, the balanced structure of traditional Christian doctrine. And the point that has to be emphasized is this: that precisely what Hooker and Andrewes, and their later followers—Jeremy Taylor, Sanderson, Thorndike, and the rest—were concerned to accomplish in the realm of doctrine, was accomplished in the realm of worship and day-to-day conduct by the lives and examples of another group of devout Churchpeople, of whom Nicholas Ferrar and his family were perhaps the most practical and, in a sense, the most influential. One quality is common to the lives of Nicholas himself, of George Herbert, Lady Falkland, Edmund Duncon and others of that time whom we could name—the character, so rare and so unmistakable when it is encountered, of personal sanctity.

It was this group of Anglican Churchpeople who, in the different circumstances of their lives, recovered for the Church of England a sense of the meaning of liturgical worship. It was they who took the Book of Common Prayer, interpreted it, and, without any self-consciousness, showed for the first time how it should be used.

The rule of Little Gidding in regard to common worship was based entirely upon the Prayer Book. The daily offices were recited with absolute regularity in church; on Sundays mattins was followed by the ante-communion office (called the " second service "), which, in the progressive collapse of liturgical worship during the reign of Elizabeth, had become the normal service on those Sundays when there were " none disposed to communicate with the priest ",—that is, on probably something like fifty out of the fifty-two Sundays in the year in most village churches. Nicholas and his friends could not and did not fail to recognize this condition of affairs for what it was, a shocking declension from any possible precedent of traditional Christian worship; and it was a great joy to him to be able to restore a monthly celebration of the Eucharist and to see his nephew, Joshua Mapletoft, with his encouragement, doing the same in Joshua's parish of Margaretting. At Little Gidding the Reverend Luke Groose, vicar of Great Gidding, was the usual celebrant and Nicholas acted as deacon.

The short hourly services in the house were ordered on a liturgical basis, with the singing of hymns, readings from the Gospels and the recitation of appointed psalms. During the night watches, which were kept from 9 p.m. till 1 a.m., the practice was to recite the whole of the psalter straight through from beginning to end, part of the office being often sung to the organ, tuned low so as not to disturb other members of the household. Nicholas, as is well known, had a special devotion to the psalter. He had learnt the whole book of psalms by heart in quite early boyhood and constantly encouraged others to do the same; " No man, till he has tried ", he used to say, " can imagine the comforts and pleasures that he may derive from such a good treasure in his heart." Verses of the psalms were constantly upon his lips. Each morning the children of the household came to him to repeat some short passage that they had learnt the previous day. It was doubtless by his encouragement that Mrs Ferrar learnt the whole psalter by heart in the later years of her life; and we know that Mary and Anna Collett and other members of the family could repeat the psalms and the greater part of the New Testament without book.

This emphasis upon liturgical forms of worship and private prayer was in part a reaction from the vagaries of sectarian individualism and from the extravagant forms of extemporary devotions. On this matter Nicholas once expressed the view that " for extemporary prayers, they needed little other confutation of them than to take them in short-hand and show them after-time to those very men that had been so audacious to vent them.   Ask them their own judgments of them (for I think they will hardly know them again) and see if they do not blame them."

It is a just and searching criticism, but one sometimes wonders whether Nicholas did not over-emphasize the value of set forms of prayer, especially in private devotion; so far as we can follow his spiritual teaching, he seems to have felt that the life of the soul could be sustained and the soul itself raised to the fulness of contemplation by the mere use of vocal prayer.   This, of course, is in accord with the belief and practice of Christian antiquity, when, as Fr Baker says:

" Many holy souls did attain to perfect contemplation by the use of vocal prayers; the which ", he adds, " would have the same effect upon us if we would or could imitate them, both in such wonderful solitude or abstraction, rigorous abstinences, and incredible assiduity in praying." *

To this Nicholas might perhaps have answered that it is precisely our duty to emulate the heroic devotion of the primitive saints, so that our spoken prayers may indeed avail to raise our hearts to the freedom of contemplation.   But there can be no doubt, as Fr Baker goes on to point out in the same passage, that in the conditions of the active life the use of private vocal prayer, though it can never be discontinued and is indeed the foundation of any act of prayer whatsoever, is yet to be regarded as a normal prelude or introduction to the more interior forms of prayer, which may, in their turn, lead the soul on to the threshold of contemplation.   Spiritual progress, therefore, will ordinarily be accompanied by a diminishing use of set forms of prayer and by greater freedom and simplicity in the interior life.   Set forms, from being a support, may become a cramping influence, hindering the full surrender of the soul to the actions and graces of the Holy Spirit.

It is not clear that Nicholas was familiar with these principles; and it may be that he would not have accepted them if he had been.   However that may be, we do find that at least one of those who looked to him for spiritual direction occasionally found his advice difficult to understand and accept.   This was Arthur

* *Holy Wisdom*, p. 344.

Woodnoth, who in one of his letters asks Nicholas to consider, " whether you do not ascribe too much to the very bodily exercises of devotion and religion. . . . I observe on all occasions that you set a high value on the very saying of prayers and other outward performances." *

From the whole tone of the long and regular correspondence between the two men and from our knowledge of their relationship, we can be sure that Arthur would not have written like this unless he had been in real perplexity. He had the sense that he was being, so to say, spiritually strait-jacketed; he would have welcomed, and surely profited by, some instruction on the interior forms of prayer and would have been led thereby into greater liberty of soul.

The truth is, I think, that there was, as yet, no adequate tradition of spiritual teaching in the Anglican Church. In that sense, Nicholas and other English Churchmen of his time were living in a vacuum. They had not been brought into any contact with the new spirituality of the Continent; as yet they knew nothing of the lives and teaching of St Teresa, St John of the Cross, St Vincent de Paul, St Francis de Sales, and other great regenerators of the Catholic Church in Europe. It is true that Nicholas was very widely read and had had the advantages of five years' residence in Italy and Spain; he was one of the least insular of men. But, in the circumstances of the time, the spiritual isolation of the Church of England was inevitable; and its recovery of tradition was therefore bound to be, in some measure, an academic and empirical process, based upon the reading of books, the study of history and practical experiment. It is this, perhaps, that explains the curious gaps in the professional equipment of the great Caroline Churchmen and the somewhat nebulous quality that occasionally appears in their teaching.

They knew themselves, of course, to be steering a middle course between Popery and Puritanism, both of which they regarded as novelties. But, as Dean Church pointed out,† it

* Magdalene College, Ferrar MSS; Arthur Woodnoth to Nicholas Ferrar, 22 August 1633.
† *Pascal and Other Sermons*, p. 98.

would be a too facile simplification of the facts to regard the development of Anglican thought and practice in this period as a mere *via media*. It was no mere compromise between two opposing extremes, but rather a genuine synthesis, worked out with a good deal of improvisation, but reposing upon real scholarship and a deliberate appeal to primitive Christianity. Its protagonists could not escape the intellectual and emotional tensions involved in its championship. Its enemies, in the fulness of their power, laid waste to Little Gidding, brought the primate of all England to the scaffold and the King himself to a martyr's death. And the foreshadowings of what was to come were clearly apparent throughout the reign of Charles I. Nicholas Ferrar, in the words of his friend Barnabas Oley, was like a man torn apart as by wild horses or ground between the upper and nether millstones of contrary opinion. He was diversely accused of being both a Papist and a Puritan; and he once declared that to fry on a faggot was not a worse torment than the continual obloquy to which he and his family had been exposed.

He was sufficiently a man of his time to assert his firm belief that the Pope was Antichrist and he once said that, if he knew that Mass had been said in a room in his house, he would have that room pulled down and rebuilt. We must not allow our natural repugnance to the crudity of these expressions to lead us to ill-considered criticism. They were mere symptoms of a general hysteria by which no man in that age was wholly un-affected. Behind it lay a century of bitter conflict, hatred, misunderstanding, mutual provocation and political rivalry—a convulsion of immense complexity in which countless factors were involved, in which every human motive from the highest to the most degraded played its part, and the rights and wrongs which, as Dom Gregory Dix says, only God can assess with both justice and mercy.*

The Ferrars certainly did not share the uncompromising prejudice of most of their contemporaries against the Roman Church. They were on terms of friendship with a neighbouring Roman Catholic family, almost certainly the Prices of Washingley Hall,

* *The Shape of the Liturgy*, p. 637.

three miles from Gidding. Nicholas himself, though he was always firm in his condemnation of what he regarded as Romanist errors, observed a careful charity in his judgements and inculcated the same in others. One comes across examples of this spirit of tolerance time and again in the records of the " Little Academy "; here, for instance, is the concluding passage of a discourse by " The Patient " (Anna Collett) on the last illness and death of Philip II of Spain:

" This was the end of that great Monarch, whose Devotion that it was not righter sett in many particulars deserves, methinks, rather tears than censures; but even where he went most wrong himself, there perhaps he may most confirm us in the truth. But leaving him to God's mercy touching his soul's estate, I wish that the remembrance of his acknowledgement touching this world's vanities may ever remain fresh in mine own and all your minds." *

It is sufficient to remember that this was spoken of the man who, scarcely more than a generation previously, had launched the Armada against England. In the *Story Books* the papal office is always spoken of with respect; in one passage, to give an instance, the two sixteenth-century Popes, Adrian VI and Marcellus II, are described as " both of them for wisdom, learning and integrity passing any of that rank that went before them many hundreds of years ", an interesting, if rather sweeping judgement. It is not the kind of language in which one would ordinarily speak of Antichrist.

So open-minded and charitable a spirit was rare in Caroline England. Indeed, a statement of Peckard's, though it is phrased with a delicious and doubtless unconscious ineptitude, does express the exact truth:

" Though they [the Ferrars] ", he says, " were pious and firm members of the Church of England, they behaved themselves quietly and with Christian benevolence towards all men of all denominations." †

It was from the Puritan side that the greatest provocation

* *Story Books of Little Gidding* (ed. E. Crwys Sharland), p. 54.
† P. Peckard, *Memoirs of Nicholas Ferrar*, p. 238.

B

came. The family were always punctiliously charitable in their judgements of Puritan conduct. Shorthouse's "Mr Thorne" in *John Inglesant* is a fictitious character, but his relationship with the Little Gidding household is in perfect accord with the historical background of the story. But Nicholas, who set the greatest store by dignity and seemliness in public worship and was strict in his loyalty to the Prayer Book rubrics, had no use at all for the way in which the Puritans tampered with the liturgy and disregarded its prescriptions. He would always, for example, wear his hood and surplice in saying the offices in church. Behind this and other observances lay his conviction that the Church of England was no newly founded Protestant sect, but an integral part of the one Catholic and Apostolic Church; and that the Anglican liturgy was no sectarian collection of prayers, but an authentic expression of the traditional intentions of Christian public worship, now for the first time written in English.

The same conviction inspired the repair and adornment of the church of Little Gidding, which was converted within a year or two from a condition of utter dereliction to one of surpassing beauty. Every member of the household, under Mrs Ferrar's general direction, had a share in the work of restoration. The church was newly floored and panelled throughout. The ancient brass font and eagle-lectern were restored in their proper places. Two complete sets of altar-frontals, cushions, carpets, desk-covers and so forth were provided, the one in sky-blue for use on Sundays and the other in green for weekdays. The stalls and benches on either side of the nave were backed with taffeta, with cushions of tapestry and silk, fringed with lace or silver. For the worthier rendering of chants and hymns a gallery was built at the west end of the church to take an organ. At the east end the cedar-wood altar stood upon a magnificent carpet of silk embroidered with gold, covering the whole sanctuary.

In the nostrils of contemporary Puritans all this had a most sulphurous reek, stinking of Popery and the pit; and it was from Puritan quarters that there came the long series of venomous and malicious slanders which reached their climax in the publication of *The Arminian Nunnery*. But the opposition between the spirit of Little Gidding and Puritanism was far more radical than any disagreement about matters of ceremonial. There was a fundamental difference of religious outlook. The best of the Puritan leaders were men of zeal and piety; they had a most lively and salutary sense of human sinfulness and of the peremptory need of penitence and contrition before man could fitly approach God at all. To them the fear of the Lord was both the beginning and the crown of wisdom; but they had an imperfect awareness that " perfect love casteth out fear ". The God of the Puritans was the God of the Old Testament rather than the New; and consequently there runs through all their teaching a radical grimness which can degenerate into a sour and arrogant pessimism.

What was lacking in Puritanism and what was the conspicuous quality in the life and spirit of Little Gidding was, quite simply, joy, that supernatural joy which is the very essence of true devotion, which rests in the knowledge of God's infinite mercy in utter simplicity of heart and lives in the consciousness of His innumerable benefits to us and to all men, a joy deep and serene, peaceful and untroubled, altogether unaffected by the trials and troubles of this present life. If we would understand the place that joy should hold in the life of the Christian, we need only consider that the early fathers of the Church counted sadness or despondency as one of the capital sins : and as a corollary we may recall the dictum of St Francis de Sales that " sadness is always unprofitable and in contradiction to the service of God ".

Now the whole tenor of life at Little Gidding was irradiated by precisely this quality of Christian joy. This was what most deeply impressed those friends and relations and casual visitors who stayed there. They were tranquillized, refreshed and infected by its presence; it was like a benediction shed abroad in the hearts of all who came. In the early spring of 1628 Nicholas was called to London for a few days on some business matter, and his mother, in writing to him, mentioned that Hester and Margaret Collett were unwell and evidently expressed some anxiety about it.

" The good that we enjoy ", wrote Nicholas in his reply, " is so far above our deserts that these lighter afflictions ought not any way to abate from our thankfulness and cheerfulness in God; but rather to count it exceeding joy that our worldly rejoicing is thus tempered and alloyed, lest it should oversprout in leaves rather than in fruit. That we have such store of God's blessings, wherewith we may the better and more easily serve God, is almost an unparalleled happiness. But it adds both to the worth and assurance of God's favour that we have withal these often remembrances, by infirmities and otherwise, to make us acknowledge the Author and to be careful to use the benefits themselves aright." *

I have observed elsewhere that the joy of Little Gidding, the joy that runs through George Herbert's poems and through Nicholas's own letters, was a thing of deep significance. It was the recovery of something that English religion had been in danger of losing altogether; it was a note that had not been heard in English devotional writing, a quality that had not been displayed in English religious life, for something like a hundred years.

There is one final point on which it is worth saying a concluding word. The rule of Little Gidding—and this, again, is a matter on which I have touched in another place—was in no sense monastic in origin or purpose. Nicholas had no intention whatever of restoring the Religious Life in the Anglican Church. Had he wished to do so, he would certainly have proceeded on quite different lines; as it was, he was quick to correct anyone who spoke of Little Gidding as a religious foundation in the technical sense of the term. He shared to the full the contemporary Anglican distrust of monasticism and when an enquirer used the word " nuns " in speaking of the Collett sisters, he took him up sharply and declared that name to be " odious ". It is only too easy to romanticize Little Gidding and to read into the narratives of Nicholas's life ideas and motives that belong to a later and more developed period of Anglican thought; and it seems certain that the suggestion sometimes made that Little Gidding represents

* Magdalene College MSS; Nicholas Ferrar to his mother, 12 March 1628.

the first effort to restore the monastic life within the Church of England is a romantic misunderstanding of this kind. By the same token, it is easy to ascribe to Nicholas a firmer grasp and a deeper knowledge of the theology of the sacraments than he in fact possessed; for this development the Church of England had to wait for another generation and more.

The truth, the very glorious truth, about the story of Little Gidding can be quite simply stated. It was essentially a family affair—a way of life adopted by members of a family, " purposing and convenanting between themselves," as Hacket expressed it, " to live in as strict a way, according to the Gospel of Christ, as good rules could chalk out and human infirmity undergo ".*

It was undertaken in an entirely private manner. It was a life of poverty voluntarily embraced, of incessant labour for the spiritual and temporal welfare of others, of practical charity, of constant prayer, with a strict regard for the fasts prescribed by the Church and cast within the framework of the forms of public worship provided in the Book of Common Prayer. It was a life in which persons of all ages took their part, a vigorous family life in which children grew up healthily and happily. As such, it is a pattern and an inspiration to be cherished and venerated, a pattern for all who are concerned to know the true ideal of Christian family life and the way in which all the circumstances of such a life may be disposed to the greater glory of God.

" In His tabernacle and in His holy sanctuary will I serve Him," Nicholas had declared when his future vocation first became clear to him, " and shall account the lowest place in His house better and more honourable than the greatest crown in the world."

His whole life, culminating in the twelve years that he spent at Gidding, was given to the fulfilment of that solemn resolve.

* *Scrinia Reserata*, Part II, p. 50.

I

THE story of Little Gidding does not end with the death of Nicholas Ferrar on that Advent Sunday in the year 1637. The dying injunction of Nicholas to his family that they should continue in the " good old way " that he had taught them was most dutifully obeyed. It was during the years immediately following his death that the great series of scriptural harmonies were planned and executed by his nephew, the younger Nicholas. The outbreak of the Civil War brought perils and anxieties which were to test their endurance to the uttermost. Of these Nicholas had warned them: John Ferrar often recalled that day, very shortly before the onset of Nicholas's last illness, when they had been walking together in the parlour at Little Gidding. Suddenly Nicholas had taken him by the hand and begun to speak in terms of passionate urgency. He had told John of his own approaching death; he had recalled all that he had taught them of the true service of God and the " right and good way that leadeth to the life everlasting ". And then he had gone on to warn him of sad times coming.

" You will live to see them, but be courageous and hold you fast to God with humility and patience, rely upon His mercy and power; you will suffer much, but God will help you: you will be sifted and endeavour will be made to turn you out of the right way, the good way you are in, even by those whom you least think of, and your troubles will be many; but be you stedfast and call upon God, and He in His good and due time will help you. Keep on your daily prayers and let all be done in sincerity, setting God always before your eyes."

No, the story does not end with Nicholas's death; and it seems worth while to assemble the surviving evidence, drawn from a variety of sources, so as to present a narrative of the last twenty years of John Ferrar's life, of those years, so full of trial and sorrow, which lay between Nicholas's death in 1637 and the death of John in old age almost exactly twenty years later. There are gaps in the story and they are gaps that can never be filled. But a sequence of events can be traced; continuity is not broken. The old way of devotion and good works was stedfastly maintained; it is another splendid and heroic chapter in the annals of the Church of England, even if it has something of the character of an epilogue.

Let us for a moment go on to the end of that span of years, for there was a certain dramatic finality about the course of things in the autumn of 1657. John Ferrar's son had been married in the summer and had decided to make his home with his wife's people in Lincolnshire. The younger Collett sisters had fulfilled the hopes always entertained for them by marrying clergymen and were dispersed to their various vicarages and rectories. Of the original household of more than thirty there were now left but six persons.

And then the final curtain descended swiftly. John Ferrar died on 28 September, Mrs Collett on 9 October, and her daughter Susanna (widow of Joshua Mapletoft) on 31 October. Early in November Bathsheba Ferrar, so recently widowed, ill and in no fit condition to travel, left Little Gidding for good, to spend the remaining two years of her life at her brother's home in London. Within a few months Mary Collett had gone too; her small income was insufficient to maintain her at Gidding and she went to her brother Thomas's house at Highgate. Only Virginia Ferrar remained; and when the younger John Ferrar, her brother, came back to Gidding to succeed his father as lord of the manor, Virginia took up residence at another house on the estate. From that time the character of the family history changes; the real Little Gidding is no more.

The death of Nicholas Ferrar in 1637 had been an almost unbearable grief and shock to the family. What should become of the poor sheep, John had despairingly asked during Nicholas's last illness, if the shepherd be taken from them? The question had come from his innermost heart, and his words, spoken within the hearing of the dying man, had drawn an immediate rebuke.

Yet John could not help himself. He had loved and revered
Nicholas with his whole being. How was it possible for the
ordered life of the household to be maintained without Nicholas
to direct it? How could the daily offices in church, the night
watches, the planning of the concordances, the instruction of the
children, the dispensing of medicines, the relief of distress among
the country folk, the hallowed cycle of worship in the house
itself—how could these things be duly continued? John had
been accustomed to consult Nicholas about all his own difficulties
and worries, and had been utterly content to defer to his judgement in everything. Was he strong enough to stand upon his
own feet after these years of reliance upon his brother's superior
wisdom and force of character? He would do his best, of course,
but the prospect filled him with apprehension. He could look
for little support or encouragement from his wife in shouldering
the new responsibilities that must now be his; Bathesheba had
no enthusiasm for the religious life of the community, though
perhaps he would find her less unsympathetic when Nicholas,
whose ascendency over her husband she had so bitterly resented,
was no longer with them. And along with Nicholas's inspiring
exhortation to continue in the " good old way ", he recalled his
brother's warnings of the trials that would assuredly come:
" There would be sad times coming ", Nicholas had declared,
" and very sad; God will bring punishments upon this land,
but, I trust, not to the utter ruin of it." For already the storm-
clouds were gathering and it was evident to clear-sighted men that
only a miracle could avert civil war.

Within a year of Nicholas's death the family suffered a second
bereavement. We do not know the circumstances in which
Anna Collett, the younger of the " maiden sisters ", died. Her
will was proved in the Archidiaconal Court of Huntingdon in
December 1638 and her uncle John Ferrar was sole executor.
Anna is one of the most lovable of all the Little Gidding characters—gentle and patient in all her ways, utterly pure in heart,
joyous in the fulfilment of her chosen vocation. Since she had
come to Gidding thirteen years earlier, she and her elder sister
Mary had worked together in complete harmony and had under-

taken many of the most responsible tasks in the ordering of the community's life. They had had charge, under Nicholas's supervision, of the dispensary and the instruction of the " psalm-children "; they did a great deal of the exquisite needlework and embroidery for which Little Gidding was to become famous; in the preparation of the concordances they were responsible for the cutting-out, pasting, and arrangement of the sacred texts and for much of the decoration: they sustained leading parts in the remarkable family study-circle known as the " Little Academy ". Both sisters, as John Mapletoft expressed it, " died Virgins, resolving so to live when they were young, by the grace of God ". It is probable, but not certain, that this resolve was ratified later by formal vows; there can be no doubt that Mary and Anna regarded themselves as solemnly pledged to singleness. To Nicholas they stood, by an agreement made between them, in the relationship of spiritual children, a relationship that was sustained in perfect mutual trust and the most tender affection.

It is clear that Mary was the stronger character of the two. Anna was quiet and self-effacing; her character of " the Patient " in the Little Academy fitted her perfectly. Hers was a life devoted to God's service, a life into which ill health brought much suffering, for Anna was subject to those recurrent malarial attacks from which Nicholas himself was never free for long. Yet her sufferings were joyously borne and transmuted into the pure gold of sanctity by the fire of divine love. Her early death at the age of thirty-four must have been a bitter grief to the family.

For John Ferrar an even greater sorrow was in store. Less than eighteen months later, in May 1640, his son Nicholas was taken from him after a short illness. Of this brilliantly talented young man, whom his uncle Nicholas had always regarded as his spiritual heir " to whom Gidding, by God's blessing, would in the end descend " and whom his father cherished with a touching admixture of pride and affection, it is fitting that we should speak rather fully; for some of his most remarkable achievements date from that short period of two and a half years between his uncle Nicholas's death and his own decease on his twentieth birthday. It is certain that his death was one of the decisive events in the

history of Little Gidding.*   Thirteen of the famous scriptural
Harmonies are known to survive at the present time; it is probable that twelve of them were actually completed during the
younger Nicholas's lifetime, and the thirteenth, the great volume
of the Pentateuch, the "gallantest, glorious, largest Booke"
of which we shall speak again in a moment, was certainly
planned by him and could not have been put in hand by anyone
else.

Nicholas Ferrar junior was born in 1620 and came to Little
Gidding with his parents as a child of five years old.   It was
apparent from the first that he was a boy of quite unusual promise.
He showed remarkable aptitude in his earliest studies and his
uncle Nicholas made himself responsible for his education,
delighting to find in him a quickness of mind and a retentiveness
of memory that made instruction an inspiring task for both of
them.   His contemporary and fellow-pupil was his cousin
Ferrar Collett; and as the two boys grew older, their uncle was
able to interest them in his own studies and exercises, so that soon
they were helping him actively in preparing a harmony of the
Gospels and other devotional works.   They shared in the
religious life of the household and, as soon as they were old
enough, would often join their uncle in the night watch, which
was maintained from 9 p.m. till 1 a.m.

The younger Nicholas cannot have been physically robust
and it may be, as Peckard suggests, that the strict self-discipline
that he imposed upon himself—"from childhood", it was to be
recorded in his epitaph, "he served God by frequent prayers,
fastings, vigils and continual self-control"—seriously overtaxed
his strength.   However that may be, his was one of those rare
spirits that was to burn itself out in the brief space of twenty
years, consuming itself by the sheer ardour and brilliancy of its
own fire.   Few men of learning have accomplished in a long
lifetime what this young man achieved before reaching his
majority.

* The reader is referred to the Reverend C. Leslie Craig's fascinating
study *Nicholas Ferrar Junior* (Epworth Press, 1950), in which much new
material is brought to light.

The story of how the first Gospel harmonies came to be compiled at Little Gidding has been often related.*   It will be remembered that, in order to provide a framework for the family's short
hourly devotions, Nicholas Ferrar made an arrangement of the
four Gospels in a single narrative;   that the volume was put
together, illustrated and bound by members of the household
working under his direction;   that the King came to hear about
the book, asked leave to borrow it and, after keeping it for several
months, returned it with the request that a similar harmony might
be made by the family for his own use.   This was in 1631;
the new harmony, a splendid volume bound in morocco, much
more elaborate than the original, was completed and presented to
the King in 1635, and is now in the British Museum.   John
Ferrar describes the delight with which the sovereign received his
gift; Charles had asked many questions concerning the manner in
which it had been compiled and which members of the family had
had a hand in it.

" Truly, my lords," he had declared to those with him, " I
prize this as a rare and rich jewel and worthy a king's acceptance.
. . . I very much thank them all, and it shall be my vade-mecum.
How happy a king were I if I had many more such work men and
women in my kingdom !   God's blessing on their hearts and
painful hands ! "

And he had gone on to ask that they should now make for him
a harmony of the books of Kings and Chronicles, a task which,
he said, he had suggested to his chaplains, but which they had
found too difficult.   The Kings–Chronicles harmony was at
once undertaken at Little Gidding and was finished and sent to
His Majesty in 1637.   It was the last harmony to be completed
during Nicholas Ferrar's lifetime.

Before long a further commission was received from the royal
household.   Prince Charles, the future Charles II, had so much
admired his father's harmony of the Gospels that he had asked
for it as a gift.   The King refused, declaring that he used the

* The most recent study of the subject is Craig's important paper,
" The Earliest Little Gidding Concordance " (*Harvard Library Bulletin*,
Autumn 1947, pp. 311–31).

book daily himself and suggesting that, if the Prince desired one of his own, those good people of Little Gidding might be willing to provide one. The intimation was accordingly conveyed by letter; Nicholas Ferrar had died some months previously, and the task of planning the new harmony fell upon his nephew. There were, it is true, ample precedents to guide him; in the preparation of the cuttings, the decoration of the sheets and the binding, tooling and so forth he had the help of Mary Collett and other members of the family. But the master-mind was his; no other would have been capable of what was to be accomplished.

" And so, in the name of God, after all materials were provided and ready, they uniting their heads and hands lovingly together, setting apart so many hours in the forenoons and so many in the afternoons, as their other exercises and occasions permitted, constantly met in a long fair spacious room, which they named the concordance chamber, wherein were large tables round the sides of the walls . . . and two very large and great presses, which were turned with iron bars, for the effecting of their designs." *

From quite early boyhood the younger Nicholas's special talent had lain in the study of languages. His gifts as a linguist were nothing short of prodigious and we shall see in a moment some of the ways in which those gifts were to be applied. In producing the harmony for Prince Charles, it was decided to introduce a new feature, a parallel narrative in four languages; this idea, as Mr Craig points out, must have originated in the mind of the younger Nicholas. The result was the magnificent volume known as the " Monotessaron ", bound in green velvet and stamped with fleurs-de-lys and sprays of oak in elaborate patterning. Its full title was as follows:

" The actions, doctrines and other passages touching our Lord and Saviour Jesus Christ, as they are related by the Four Evangelists; harmonically, symmetrically and collaterally placed in four languages, English, Latin, French, Italian, reduced into one

* John Ferrar. His narrative (Lambeth Palace MS 251) is printed in Wordsworth's *Ecclesiastical Biography*, Vol. V, and in Mayor's *Two Lives*.

complete body of history; wherein that which is severally related by them is digested into order and that which is jointly related by all or any of them is first extracted into one narration, by way of composition; secondly, brought into one clear context by way of collection; to which are, in all the pages of the book, added sundry of the best pictures that could be gotten, expressing the facts themselves or their types, figures or other matters appertaining thereunto; done at Little Gidding, anno 1640."

When this great work was brought to completion, it was felt in the family that its actual presentation to the Prince was a somewhat delicate matter. The younger Nicholas recalled an oft-repeated injunction of his uncle's, that it was never fitting to make a present to any person whomsoever without the previous knowledge and consent of that person's superior. It was accordingly decided that, before the great " Monotessaron " could fitly be given to the Prince, it must first be shown to and approved by his father. Further reflection suggested the corollary that it might appear ungracious to make this approach to the King without having a gift for him also; and work was started at once upon two volumes to be presented at the same time to the King, a single Gospel translated into eight languages and a New Testament translated into twenty-four. It was in no spirit of vanity that Nicholas put in hand a third task. He wished to be able to demonstrate that he did really understand the languages used and had not merely copied the texts from other versions. The third volume was intended to establish his linguistic knowledge beyond possibility of doubt; it was to be, as his father described it, a " proufe book " and was to be kept in reserve in case of need. These three books, we should understand, were different in character from the harmonies, in whose compilation a number of persons could collaborate, in preparing and pasting in the cuttings, arranging the illustrations and so forth; these were manuscript volumes and must be regarded substantially as the unaided work of Nicholas.

When all was completed, the four volumes were shown to the Bishop of Peterborough and to certain learned scholars in Cambridge to judge of their merit and fittingness for presentation to the King. All expressed their admiration; and so there came a great day when Nicholas, accompanied by his father, travelled up to London to be received at Whitehall and to present his gifts. It was the Wednesday in Holy Week in the year 1640. They went by appointment to Lambeth Palace, where Laud gave them an affectionate welcome. Nicholas knelt for the Archbishop's blessing and then, at his request, displayed his books. Laud was warm in his commendation; he asked many questions and kept the young man in conversation for some time. Then he dismissed him, bidding him attend on the afternoon of the following day, being Maundy Thursday, in a certain room in Whitehall Palace.

The Archbishop met them and took them at once into an adjoining room, where the King was standing by the fire with several noblemen. Nicholas knelt to kiss the King's hand and then drew out from his box the book, the " Monotessaron ", that had been made for the Prince. The King turned its pages and expressed his delighted appreciation: " Here is a fine book for Charles indeed ! I hope it will soon make him in love with what is within it; for I know it is good." Then Nicholas, being invited to speak, explained that he would not have made bold to present the volume to the Prince without His Majesty's consent and approval; whereupon the King turned to the Archbishop and enjoined that on the morrow Nicholas should travel to Richmond, where the Prince was lodged, to make the presentation, " It is a good day, you know, and a good work would be done upon it."

Nicholas now produced the first of the books intended for the King and craved his acceptance of it. It was the Gospel in eight languages and as Charles took and began to peruse it with eager admiration, the Archbishop observed: " When your majesty hath seen all, you will have more cause to admire ".

"What," said the King, " is it possible we shall behold yet more rarities? "

And, at the Archbishop's sign, Nicholas took out his next gift, the New Testament in twenty-four languages. This time the King's enthusiasm knew no bounds.

" What is this? What have we here? The incomparablest book this will be, as ever eye beheld. My lords, come, look well upon it. This must be the emperor of all books. It is the crown of all works. It is an admirable masterpeice. The world cannot match it. I believe you are all of my opinion."

The words, recorded by John Ferrar a few years after they were spoken, bring the scene vividly before us. Every incident of this amazing afternoon must have stamped itself indelibly on John's mind as he watched the King's delighted interest and heard the astonished comments of those present. The young Nicholas, deferential but by no means overawed, remained perfectly composed; and presently the conversation took precisely the course that he had anticipated.

" I observe two things amongst others," said the King, " very remarkable, if not admirable. The first is, how is it possible that a young man of twenty-one years of age should ever attain to the understanding and knowledge of more languages than he has years. . . . The other is also of high commendation, to see him write so many several languages, each in its proper character."

But there was one point, the King continued, addressing himself to the Archbishop, on which he would welcome reassurance; it was a great achievement in itself to be able to write these several scripts, but what certain evidence was there that the young man understood each language and could translate word for word into English? This was the moment for which Nicholas had been waiting; he had expected, he said, that the King in his great wisdom would propound this precise question and he had therefore prepared for the King's eyes a further work which would provide full proof of the matter, which would show that he did understand all this great range of languages and could translate them into English or Latin. He now produced from his box the volume which his father calls the " proufe " book, a fine calfbound folio which is assuredly one of the most remarkable of all the Little Gidding productions.*

* The book, which is in private hands, is fully described by Craig, op. cit., Chapter III.

Its full title is as follows:

" Sacrosanctum Scti Johannis
Evangelium
In totidem Linguis quot sunt capita
v. L.

Caput	Caput
1. Aethiopice	11. Germanice
2. Graece	12. Bohemice
3. Syriace	13. Hungarice
4. Arabice	14. Gallice
5. Latine	15. Danice
6. Saxonice	16. Italice
7. Hebraice	17. Suedice
8. Anglice	18. Hispanice
9. Cambro-brittanice	19. Polonice
10. Cantabrice	20. Belgice

21. Hibernice et Moscovitice

Et unaquaeq. Lingua per Interlinearem Latinam Interpretationem ad verbum redditam et positam explicata."

It is, in fact, an arrangement of St John's Gospel in twenty-one languages, as many languages as there are chapters. Only the opening verses of each chapter are given, a separate language for each chapter according to the schedule given above. Three texts are given throughout, first the Latin Vulgate, then immediately below it the text of the particular language in its own characters, and beneath this again, to show that the compiler fully understood each language, a transliteration into English characters.

Charles took the volume, turning the pages and studying them closely. Again he exclaimed in admiration; he called the Archbishop to the table and declared himself fully satisfied. Presently the book was being handed round amongst the company and others added their words of praise. The King was in the highest spirits.

" We have spent part of our Maundy Thursday to good purpose, have we not, my lords? "

And then, turning to young Nicholas, he told him that he wished him to go the following morning to Richmond to make his own presentation of the gift to Prince Charles.

" After the holiday ", he concluded, " return to my lord of Canterbury; and then you shall know my good approbation of yourself and all you have done."

As Nicholas and his father were taking their dismissal, the King made some observation to the Archbishop about Nicholas's stammer, " What pity is it that this youth hath not his speech altogether so ready as his pen and great understanding is!" Lord Holland put in with the suggestion that a speech-defect of this kind was often helped by carrying a small pebble in the mouth.

" Nay, nay," said the King, " I have tried that, but it helps not. I will tell him the best and surest way is to take good deliberation at first and not to be too sudden in speech.   And let him also learn to sing, that will do well." *

On the following morning, in a coach drawn by four horses and with " some other company of his friends ", Nicholas travelled down to Richmond.   Bishop Duppa, the Prince's tutor, received them; and they were then taken in and presented to Prince Charles, at that time a boy of ten years old.   The Prince received his gift very graciously.   Then his younger brother, the Duke of York, asked Nicholas to make a similar book for him.

" How long will it be before I have it ? " he enquired; and when Nicholas replied that it would be made with all good speed, the little Duke persisted: " But how long will that be?   I pray tell the gentlewomen at Gidding I will heartily thank them if they will dispatch it."   The courtiers present were much amused by the Duke's earnestness; and after Nicholas had reiterated his promise, the Princes withdrew and Bishop Duppa conducted Nicholas and his friends into another room for dinner.   At table he asked Nicholas many questions about Little Gidding;   afterwards they had conversation with some of the other noblemen, including the Duke of Buckingham.   The Prince was pleased to

* As is well known, Charles himself suffered with a stammer.

c

see Nicholas again before his departure, thanked him again " for the jewel you have given me and for the contrivement of it " and, as a testimony of his acceptance of it, gave the young man twenty golden shillings.

There was still more to come. On the Saturday morning Nicholas and his father called again on the Archbishop, who was delighted to hear of all that had passed at Richmond. He then took John Ferrar aside and acquainted him that the King had been greatly impressed both by Nicholas's remarkable gifts and by his personal qualities. His Majesty had given instructions that after the present holidays the young man should be sent up to Oxford University and should be maintained there at the royal charge.

" Assure yourself," concluded Laud, " he shall want nothing. In a word, the king is greatly in love with him; and you will and have cause (*sic*) to bless and praise God for such a son."

We must use the proud father's own words to describe the concluding scene :

" So John Ferrar being ravished with joy, in all humble manner gave thanks to my lord's grace. And they returning to Nicholas Ferrar, my lord embraced him and gave him his benediction. Nicholas Ferrar, kneeling down, took the bishop by the hand and kissed it. He took him up in his arms, laid his head to his cheek and earnestly besought God Almighty to bless him and increase all graces in him every day more and more for an instrument of His glory here upon earth and a saint in heaven, ' which,' said he, ' is the only happiness that can be desired and ought to be our chief end in all our actions. God bless you ! God bless you ! I have told your father what is to be done for you after the holidays. God will provide for you better than your father can. God bless you and keep you ! ' So they parted from his grace."

Mysterious are the ways of God's providence ; precious in the Lord's sight is the death of His saints. Nicholas had the knowledge that Easter Eve that his future was assured ; his university career was provided for and was to begin in a few weeks. On Easter Sunday morning he and his father were early at St Paul's Cathedral and received Holy Communion ; later in the day he felt unwell and had no appetite for his dinner. They went to church in the afternoon, but he was no better in the evening and on the following morning it was apparent that he was seriously ill. Two physicians were called in; they did all they could, but, as one day succeeded another, the patient grew steadily worse. Like his uncle Nicholas of blessed memory, he seemed before long to know that his sickness was unto death; and when his old friend Dr Towers, now Bishop of Peterborough, came to visit him, he declared that he was in no way troubled to die.

There came a day—it was about a month later, to be precise on 8 May—when there was rioting in London, and Lambeth Palace was assaulted by a mob of hooligans. It was told Nicholas on his sick-bed.

" Alas, alas ! " he protested, " God help His church and poor England ! I now fear indeed what my dear uncle said before he died is at hand, that evil days were coming and happy were they that went to heaven before they came. . . . God amend all ! Truly, truly it troubles me."

We have no means of judging the nature of his illness; its course was strikingly similar to that which had brought death to his uncle. His strength was by now failing and he would frequently commend himself humbly and cheerfully to God's love and mercy : " I am too young to be mine own judge what is best for me, to die or live; but let all be as God's will is." A few days later the Bishop of Peterborough gave him absolution, for it was clear that the end was near at hand.

" God give you consolation," said the Bishop to John Ferrar, " and prepare yourself to part with your good son. He will in a few hours, I think, go to a better world; for he is no way for this, that I see, by his body or by his soul. Be of good comfort; you give him but again to Him that gave him you for a season."

Two days afterwards he died, praying and calling upon God, " Lord Jesus, receive my soul ". It was on 19 May 1640, his twentieth birthday.*

* The foregoing narrative is taken from John Ferrar's account. The manuscript sources are the Lambeth MS 251, a parallel narrative in the Tangye MSS at the London Museum, and a shorter version discovered by Craig in the " Proof " Book examined and described by him. Tran-

So ended this rare and beautiful life.   A most moving tribute
to the younger Nicholas's memory was provided in a Latin
epitaph composed by his friend, Mark Frank, Fellow of Pembroke Hall, Cambridge; Mr Craig has given us an English
rendering in full.*   Here is celebrated the amazing intellectual
talent of the young scholar, to whom

> " the study of languages was a necessity
> History a relaxation,
> Philosophy a devotion,
> Mathematics a delight,
> Music a duty,
> Theology a vocation."

Here, too, we may read of his strict self-discipline in God's
service, of his obedience to his parents, his gifts of friendship, his
generosity and his deep humility of spirit.   The actual achievements of his brief life are astonishing enough; but we know from
surviving papers that he had plans for a parallel New Testament
in no fewer than fifty languages and, as we shall see, another
immense work, for whose structure and arrangement he was
himself responsible, was to be completed at Little Gidding after
his death.   It is fortunate that several of his major works have
been preserved; but the single Gospel in eight languages and
the New Testament in twenty-four, which were presented to
Charles I, have disappeared and it can hardly be hoped that they
have survived.   It has been stated that these two volumes were
later taken back to Gidding; † and we have John Ferrar's authority for saying that the book which was made for the Duke of
York was never given to him; it was still at Gidding when John

---

scripts of the Lambeth MS appear in Mayor and in Wordsworth's *Eccle-
siastical Biography*, Vol. V; the Tangye MS was transcribed in *Notes and
Queries*, 27 April 1895.   It is probable that John Ferrar wrote his longer
account in 1653 and the shorter one between then and his own death in
1657.
  * Op. cit., pp. 37–9.
  † J. E. Acland, *Little Gidding and Its Inmates in the time of Charles I*
(London, 1903), p. 60; no authority is given for the statement.

wrote in 1653.* Other harmonies, based upon earlier work carried out by the family, were made at Little Gidding during the years after the younger Nicholas's death; but it remains true that his death was a decisive landmark, for when he was gone, there was no one capable of planning further enterprises of the kind.

* Mayor, op. cit., p. 137.

II

IT was, indeed, intended that the works of the younger
Nicholas that were left unfinished should be completed by his
cousin, Ferrar Collett; and it is certain that a number of fine
volumes, based on the earlier harmonies, were produced after
Nicholas's death. St John's College, Oxford, possesses an
arrangement of the Pentateuch that was made at Little Gidding for
Archbishop Laud. We know of a harmony that was made for
Dr Thomas Jackson, Dean of Peterborough, and of a Kings–
Chronicles concordance for Bishop Wharton. For some of these
later volumes a remuneration was accepted; John Ferrar says
that the family received £37 for the Wharton concordance.
Apart from these enterprises, a good deal of fine decorative book-
binding was undertaken—Bibles, Prayer Books, and devotional
works, such as the copy of St Francis de Sales's *Introduction to the
Devout Life*, which Dr Basire gave to his future wife and which,
he tells her, was " bound by those virgins I once told you of.
Who knows but the prayers they might bestow at the binding
may do you good at the reading? " *

But all work of this kind was becoming increasingly difficult.
By the summer of 1640 the air was sultry with the gathering threat
of war. The enemies of Little Gidding were becoming bolder.
Libellous rumours were in constant circulation about the family
and their way of life, and threats of open violence were becoming
more frequent. Some time during 1641 Bishop Williams
conducted his last visitation of the diocese and came once more to
Little Gidding. He had been Bishop of Lincoln for twenty
years; and since the Ferrars had first come to Gidding in 1625,
he had been to them a true father in God. Constantly and
energetically he had protected them against their critics; in his
actions as bishop he had gone out of his way to show his admiration for their piety and devotion; with Nicholas Ferrar he had

* Peckard, op. cit., pp. 209, 272; Mayor, op. cit., pp. 149, 243, 361.

been on terms of most affectionate friendship. It is indeed a wonderful tribute to the Little Gidding household, and to the place that they occupied in the Anglican Church, that they were held in equally high regard by those two great Churchmen, Laud and Williams, who were such implacable rivals in the ecclesiastical politics of the time.

In the immense memorial biography of Williams by his former chaplain, John Hacket, there is an attractive passage about Little Gidding which is not well known, and is, I think, worth transcribing.* It takes us back several years, to the days when old Mrs Ferrar was still alive, and it can be assumed that Hacket had much of his information from the bishop himself. He would have found some of his material amongst Williams's papers—the report of the formal visit; perhaps a copy of the inscription in the parlour at Gidding; a draft of the " Judgment on Three Sheets of paper " dealing with the intended vows of Mary and Anna Collett; and so on. Besides, he was himself near Gidding at the time and no doubt frequently at Buckden, so that he could easily have obtained other first-hand information.

" A Family of the *Ferrars* ", he writes, " the Mother, with Sons and Daughters of both sexes in the plural Number, other Branches of the Kindred, with Servants fit to be about them, were collected into a House of their own at *Giding* aforesaid, purposing and covenanting between themselves to live in as strict a way, according to the Gospel of Christ, as good Rules could chalk out, and humane infirmity undergo. This pious Design was proposed and perswaded to them by the eldest Son, in Holy Orders, bred in *Clare-Hall* in Cambridge, an humble, diligent, devout Servant of God, learned in the Theory, more in the Practice of Divinity. Their House, fit for their Contemplation, stood alone. All were single Persons in it, to the best I could learn. The Church was so near that it was next to the Pale of their Yard; the easier for them that frequented it so often. The whole Village of *Giding* had depopulated, or I am misinform'd: the House which contained them remaining for an whole

* John Hacket, *Scrinia Reserata : a Memorial of John Williams*, D.D. etc. (London, 1693), Part II, pp. 50–2.

Parish.   The Tythes had been impropriated: but were restored back again by the Mother, to the use of the Rector then, her own Son; and to the succeeding Rectors, by a firm Deed, as Law could make, which in its time shall be declared.   They kept much at home: their turns of Prayer, and Watching, which they observed, requir'd it.   Yet Visits, perhaps once a Month, they made abroad: but shunning such Diversions, as much as they could, which rob us of a great part of the Employment of our Life.   *Non horam tecum esse potes : non otia recte Ponere :* as an Heathen complained, *Horat.   Serm.* 7.   Strangers that came to them were fairly received: all the Tribe was meek and courteous, and did let none depart, before they gave them an account of their Conversation, if they ask'd it.   And withall offer'd to read to them, what was written in a Table hanging up in their Parlour, as followeth:

" *He that by report of our Endeavours, will remonstrate that which is more perfect, and seek to make us better, is welcome as an Angel of God.   He that by chearful participating, and approbation of that which is good, confirms us in the same, is welcome as a Christian friend.   He that any way goes about to divert, or disturb us in that which is, as it ought to be among Christians (though it be not usual in the World) is a Burthen while he stays, and shall bear his judgment whosoever he be.   He that faults us in absence for that which in presence he made shew to approve, shall by a double guilt of Flattery and Slander, violate the Bands both of Friendship, and Christianity.*

" *Subscribed,*

" *MARY FARRAR, Widow, Mother of this Family, aged Fourscore Years : who bids adieu to all Hopes and Fears of this World, and only desires to serve God.*

" Their Apparel had nothing in it of Fashion, but that which was common: yet plain: and much of it for Linnen and Woollen spun at home; such as modest Christians thought to be the best habit.   *Fateor vobis de pretiosa veste erubesco,* says St. Austin.   *Inter serm. de diver.*   They gave no entertainment, but to the Poor, whom they instructed first, and then relieved, not with Fragments, but with the best they had: and having sufficiency

did abound to every good work. 2 *Cor.* 11.8. Their business
was, either they were at Prayer, or at work: nothing came
between: the Devil had the less Power to tempt them, that he
never found them idle. They had the more leisure for work,
because they fasted so much: and their diet at their meals was
soon drest; besides, their daily temperance was such, as they
sat not long at them. It was not by fits, but by constancy, that
they subdued their Bodies by Sobriety. Their Bread was
coarse, their Drink small, and of ill Relish to the Taste: that it
was sure they strived for nothing, that a dainty Appetite might
long for. As Alms and Fasting were frequent with them, so
Prayers and Watching, with Reading and Singing Psalms, were
continually in their Practice. *Note*, The word continually: For
there was no Intermission, day, nor night. Four times every
day they offer'd up their Supplications to God, twice in the
Words of the Common-Prayer in the Church: twice in their
Family, with several Petitions for their own needs, or for such as
desired, upon some special occasions, to be remembered by them
to God. At all times one, or more, by their Constitutions were
drawn aside to some private Holy Exercise. By night they kept
watch in the House of the Lord, and two by turns did supply
the Office for the rest, from which they departed not till the
Morning. Their Scope was to be ready like wise Virgins with
Oil in their Lamps, when the Bridegroom came. This was the
hardest part of their Discipline, that they kept Centinel at all
Hours and Seasons, to expect the second coming of the Lord
Jesus. . . . God to be glorified for such, whose Prayers were
powerful and uncessant to pierce the Heavens. The whole Land
was the better for their Sanctity. They fasted, that Famine
might not be inflicted upon our common Gluttony. They
abridg'd themselves of all Pleasures, that Vengeance might not
come down upon the Voluptuousness of this riotous Age. They
kept their Vigils all Night, that the Day of the Lord might not
come upon us like a thief unawares, that sleep in security. The
whole World was the better for their contempt of the World.
They were in the World, not of the World. All their Practice
was heavenly: a great deal of it had some singularity, by the

custom of our corrupt ways, who do not strive to enter in at the strait Gate, to come to Blessedness.

" The Fame of the Dispensations of this worthy Family, the further it was heard abroad, the more it sounded like Popery. Envy or Ignorance could guess no better at it, but it was a *Casa Professa*, a Convent pack'd together of some Superstitious Order beyond Sees or a Nunnery, and that the Sufferance of it look'd towards a change in Religion. . . . A Crew of Bawds and Gamesters might have set up a Standing with less prejudice than these Devotionaries.   But God help us, if the best Protestants (for these may be called so) do look like Papists.   Had they been hired with Gold, that so mistook them, they could not have done more Credit and Honour to our Adversaries.   Speak, Sir *Censurer*, we the true children of the Church of England, were we not without departing from our own Station, capable of Mortification?   of vowing ourselves to God?   of renouncing the World?   of Fasting?   of Vigils?   of prayer limited to Canons and Hours, as any that say, and do not, that call themselves from St. *Basil*, St. *Bennet*, or such Institution?   Not our Reformation, but our Slothfulness doth indispose us, that we let others run faster than we, in Temperance, in Chastity, in Scleragogy, as it was call'd.   The Diocesan, and their Neighbour to this Family in a few Miles, was asham'd at these Scandals, which he knew to be spiteful and temerarious.   He knew the Occurrences of his Precinct; as *Apelles* was wont to sit behind the Pictures hung up in his Shop, to hear what Passengers that went to and fro did approve, or discommend.   These were known to the Bishop by right Information, from the time that they sealed a Charter among themselves, as it were, to be constant and regular in their Spiritual Discipline.   But their Heavenly mindedness was best discover'd to him, when two Sons of Mrs. *Farrar*, the Mother and Matron of the Household, treated with the Bishop, to endow the Church with the Tythes, which had been impropriated: this was in *Sept.* 1633, as appears by a Smack of that which fell from the Pen of the *Donor*, as followeth:

" Right Reverend Father in God,

" *The Expectation of Opportunities, having some Years whealed*

me off from the Performance of this Business, I now think it neces-
sary to break through all Impediments, and humbly present to your
Lordship the Desires, and the Intentions of my Heart. Beseeching
you on God's behalf, to take them into your Fatherly Consideration,
and to give a speedy Accomplishment to them, by the Direction of
your Wisdom and the Assistance of your Authority.

" The rest is too much to be rehearsed, save a little of her
Prayer to God in the end of the Papers.

" *Be graciously pleased, Lord, now to accept from thy Hand-*
maid the Restitution of that, which hath been unduely heretofore
taken from thy Ministers. And as an earnest and pledge of the
total Resignation of her self, and hers to thy Service, vouchsafe to
the use of thy Church this small portion of that large Estate, which
thou hast bestowed upon her, the unworthiest of thy Servants. Lord
redeem thy Right whereof thou hast been too long disseized by the
World, both in the Possessions, and in the Person of thy Hand-
maid. And let this outward Seizure of Earth be accompanied with
an inward Surprizal of the Heart and Spirit into thine own Hands :
So that the Restorer, as well as that which is restored, may become,
and be confirmed thine Inheritance, &c.

" The Bishop pray'd to God that many such Customers might
come to him: so commended her free-will offering to God and
confirm'd it. To make them some amends for their Liberality
to the Church, he devised how to give them Reputation against
all Detraction. Therefore in the Spring that came after, he gave
them warning on what *Sunday* he would Preach in their Church:
whither an extreme Press of People resorted from all the Towns
that heard of it. In his Sermon he insisted most, what it was to
die *unto the World*: that the Righteous should scarce be saved:
that our Right Eye, and our right Hand, and all our fleshly
Contentments must be cut off, that we may enter into Life. All
tended to approve the dutiful and severe Life of the *Farrars*,
and of the Church that was in their House. After Sermon the
Bishop took their Invitation to Dine with them. But they were
so strict to keep that day holy, that they left not a Servant at
home to provide for the Table. Yet it was handsomely furnish'd
with that which was boil'd and bak'd, that requir'd no Attendance,

to stay any one from Church to look to it.   By this visit the
Bishop had the Means to see their way of serving God: to know
the Soundness of Doctrine which they maintained, to read
their Rules which they had drawn up for Fasts, and Vigils,
and large Distribution of Alms; In which he bad them proceed in the Name of God, and gave them his Blessing at his
departing.   From henceforth these faithful ones flourish'd in
good opinion.

" Yet nothing is so sound, but in time it will run into Cor-
ruption.   For I must not hold it in, that some Persons in *Little
Giding* had run into excess, and incurr'd offence, if the Bishop
had not broken the Snare, which they were preparing for their
own feet.   For after he had spoken well of the Family in the
Pulpit, and privately to divers, some of them could not see when
they were well, but aspir'd to be Transcendants above their
measure.   For two Daughters of the Stock came to the Bishop,
and offer'd themselves to be vail'd Virgins, to take upon them the
vow of perpetual Chastity, with the Solemnity of the Episcopal
Blessing and Ratification.   Whom he admonished very Fatherly,
that they knew not what they went about, that they had no
promise to confirm that Grace unto them: that this readiness,
which they had in the present, should be in their will, without
Repentance, to their Lives end.   Let the younger women marry,
was the best advice, that they might not be led into Temptation.
And that they might not forget what he taught them, he drew up
his Judgment in Three Sheets of Paper, and sent it them home,
that they might dress themselves by that Glass, and learn not to
think of Humane Nature, above that which it is, a Sea of Flowings
and Ebbings, and of all manner of Inconstancy.   The Direction
of God was in this Council: For one of the Gentlewomen
afterwards took a liking to a good husband and was well
bestowed."

Taking into account Hacket's rather special opportunities for
exact knowledge of what he was writing about, it is surprising
that his enthusiastic and, in many ways, moving description of
the " Congregation of Saints" contains so many errors.   Nicholas

was not Mrs Ferrar's eldest son, and neither of her sons was ever rector of Little Gidding. Again, John Ferrar and his wife brought up their children at Gidding, whilst Mr and Mrs Collett with their family of sixteen and, as the years passed, their steadily increasing number of grandchildren could scarcely have been more fruitfully married; yet Hacket thought that everyone in the place was celibate.

The mis-statement about the subsequent marriage of one of the Maiden Sisters is even more astonishing. As to the vows of virginity taken by Mary and Anna, his account is incomplete and, one fears, not unprejudiced.

Hacket had been Archdeacon of Bedford for a number of years when, in 1661, he was consecrated Bishop of Lichfield. His cathedral, after the years of the Commonwealth, was hardly more than a heap of ruins and he spent the remaining eight years of his life in rebuilding it. Lichfield Cathedral, as we know it to-day, is substantially his monument. He had probably completed his biography of Williams before he went to Lichfield; but the book was not published until 1693, nearly a quarter of a century after its author's death.

It was, we have said, in 1641 that Bishop Williams came to Gidding for the last time. After the formal ceremonies he sat talking in the parlour with John Ferrar, and his eye fell on that striking inscription which Nicholas and his mother had set up over the hearth a good many years previously. Williams looked at it intently and then spoke with a note of urgency in his voice.

" I shall counsel you now ", he said to John, " to take this down and let it not hang in this public room any longer. Not that I dislike it, but approve of it. The times, I fear me, as you see, grow high and turbulent, and great may be the folly and madness of the people."

He went on to describe the hostile reception he had met in his visitation of Boston and emphasized that he was not instructing John as his bishop, but advising him as a friend. They talked of old times and of Nicholas; and then, after giving his blessing to the family, the Bishop took his leave. When he had gone,

John, with a heavy heart, took the inscription down and put it away. And so, to use his own words, " The old gentlewoman's tablet was taken down out of the common parlour, whereunto indeed, not very long after, came men of another garb than the bishop's and of other minds."

III

THE Bishop's warning was a shrewd one. It cannot have been more than two or three months later that John Ferrar received further disturbing evidence of the dangers that threatened him and his household; for in the early autumn of 1641 the notorious pamphlet called *The Arminian Nunnery* was published in London.

To appreciate fully the character of this scurrilous document we must again go back for a few years, to a morning in late spring in the year 1634 (almost certainly Ascension Day) when a young barrister named Edward Lenton arrived unannounced at Little Gidding and asked to see the master of the house. He had been staying in the neighbourhood with a friend, Sir Thomas Hetley, and was going on to spend a few days at Lord Montagu's place at Kimbolton. Hetley had doubtless told him something about the Ferrars of Little Gidding, and Lenton, his interest keenly aroused, had decided to call upon them. He arrived at about 10 a.m. and stayed two hours. It was a weekday and the family were following their usual avocations.

Lenton subsequently set down his impressions of what he saw and heard in a long letter to Hetley. He was a man of intelligence and integrity; and his account is of great value, for it is the only surviving account of Little Gidding written by an outsider. Lenton makes it clear, as will be seen, that he did not approve of, or at any rate did not understand, everything that came under his notice. But his scrupulous honesty and sincerity of mind are apparent throughout.

The accompanying transcript of the letter has been made from the manuscript copy in Mary Collett's exquisite hand, preserved at Magdalene College, Cambridge. It has been exactly copied, except that abbreviations have been expanded, the narrative has been broken up into paragraphs and, for the sake of clarity, the punctuation has been modernized where it seemed desirable.

Mary Collett's script may reasonably be taken as an accurate copy of what Lenton actually wrote; and I think it is worth having made a new transcript because Peckard's version, which was used by Mayor and Wordsworth and has been taken as the accepted text by all subsequent biographers, is not quite accurate in several points. Most are unimportant; but in one case, to which reference is made in a footnote, the wrong transcription of a single word (" their " for " other ") has seriously altered the sense of what Nicholas Ferrar really said.

The text is as follows:

" The copy of my letter to Sir Tho: Hetley, Kt. and Serjeant at Lawe to Certifie him as I found.

" Good Mr. Serjeant,

" I can give you but a short account of my not two houres stay at the Reputed (at least reported) Nunnery at Gidding, and yet must leave out 3 parts of our passages as fitter for Rilacion than a letter.

" I came thither after Tenne, and found a ffaire house, ffairelier seated, to which I passed through a ffine grove, and sweete walkes, littised and gardened on both sides; their livelihood 500 li. per annum (as my Lord Mountague told me, one of his Mantion houses being within two or three miles of them). A man servant brought me into a ffaire spatious Parlor, whither (soone after) came to me the ould gentlewoman's second Sonne, a Bachelor, of a plaine presence, but of able speech and parts, who (after I had, as well as in such a case I could, deprecated any ill conceits of me for so unusuall and bold a visit) entertained me very civillye and with much humilitie, yet said I was the ffirst that ever came to them in that kind, though not the ffirst they had heard of that determined to come.

" After deprecations and some complements, he said I should see his Mother (a tall, straite, cleere complexioned grave matron of ffourscore yeares of age) his elder Brother married but whether a widdower or noe I asked not (a short black Complexioned man, his apparrell and haire soe fashioned as made him shewe Prieste like) and his sister married to one Mr. Collet, by whom she hath 14 or 15 Children, all which are in the house which I sawe not yet. And of these and 2 or 3 Maide Servants the familie consists.

" I saluted the Mother and daughter, not like Nunnes but as we use to salute other women. And after we were all sett circuler wise and my deprecations renewed to the other three, I desired, that to their favour of entertaininge me they would add the giving of me ffree libertie to speak ingenuouslie what I conceived of any thing I should see or have heard of without any distast to them, which being graunted ; I first tould them what I had heard of the Nunnes of Gidding, Of two watching and praying all night, of their Canonicall houres, of their Crosses on the outside and inside of their Chappell, of an Alter there richlie dekt with plate, Tapestry and Tapers, of their Adoracion and Geniculations at their entering therein, which, I objected, might savour of Superstition and Poperie.

" Here the younger Sonne (the Mouth of them all) cutt me of, and to this last answered ffirst, with a protestacion, That he did as verilie believe the Pope to be Antichrist as any Article of his faith, wherewith I was satisfied and silenced touching that point. For the Nunry, he said the name of Nunnes was odious, but the trewth (from whence that untrue report might arise) was that 2 of his Nieces had lived one Thirty, the other 32 years Virgins, and so resolved to continue (as he hoped they would) the better to give themselves to fasting & prayer, but had made no vowes. For their Canonicall houres, he said they usually prayed six times a day (as I remember) twice a day publickelie in their Chappell, and foure times more privatelie in their house; In the Chappell after the order of the Book of Comon Prayer, in their house particuler prayers for a private family. I said, If they spent soe much time in praying they would leave litle for Preaching or for their weeklie callings; For the one I vouched the Text He that turneth away his Eare from hearing the Lawe his prayer is abominable, for the other six dayes thou shalt labour &c. To the one he Answered, That a Neighbour Minister of another Parrish came on Sunday Mornings and preached in their Chappell, and sometimes they went to his Parrish. To the other, That their calling was to serve God, which he took to be the best.

" I replied that for men in health and of Active bodies and parts it were a tempting God to quit our callings and wholly

D

betake ourselves to prayer and fasting and a contemplative life, which by some is thought little better than a Spetious kind of Idleness, not to terme it as St. Augustine termes Morall virtues without Christ Splendida peccata; hee rejoynd, That they had found divers perplexities, distractions and almost utter ruin in other * callings, but if others knewe what content God had ministered to them since their sequestracion, and what incredible improvement of their livelihood, it might incourage others to the like course. I said that such an imitacion might be of dangerous consequence, and that if any in good case before should thereby fall into povertie, fewe afterwards would follow the example:

" For their night watchings and for their riseing at Foure a clock in the morning, which I thought was much for one of Four-score years of age and for children, To the one he said, It was not much sith they alwayes went to bed at 7 a Clock in the evening. For the other he confest there was every night two (alternatim) continued all night in their devotions that went not to bed till the rest arose. For their Crosses he made the usuall Answer, That they were not ashamed of that badge of christian profession which the First propugnors of the Faith bore in their Banners and which we in the Church discipline retaine to this day. For their Chappell, that it was now neere Chappell tyme (For eleven is the houre in the forenoon) and that I might if I pleased accompany them thither and soe satisfye my self best of which I had heard concerning that, which offer I willingly enterteyned:

" Mean tyme I told them I perceived all was not true that I had heard of the place ffor I could see no such inscription on the Frontispiece of the house contayning an invitation of such as were willing to learn of them or would teach them better, which was some incouragement to me to come (as one desirous to learn not to teach) and might be some excuse of my audacity if they would be pleased soe to accept it;

" But he (barring me from further Complement) said the ground of that Report hunge over my head. Wee sitting by the

---

* Peckard transcribed " other " as " their ", which, of course, gives a completely wrong sense to the passage. The error appears in every printed version of Lenton's letter that I know.

Chimney on the Chimney piece there was a Manuscript Tablature which after I had read I craved leave to begg a Coppy thereof, soe that they would not take me for too bold a beggar, which he forthwith took downe, and commanded to be presentlie transcripted and given to me.   I offered the writer money for his deserved paines which was refused.   And the master conjured me not to offer it the second tyme and thereupon made it his suite to me not to offer any thing to any of that house at my parting or otherwise.   The words of the protestation are as followeth.

☩

I H S

He that by reproof of our errors or Remonstrance of that which is more perfect, seekes to make us better, is welcome as an Angell of God	And	He that by a cheerfull participating in that which is good confirmes us in the same, is welcome as a Christian Friend

But

He that any waye goes about to divert or disturb us in that which is as it ought to be among Christians, though it be not usuall in the world, is a Burthen whilst he stays, and shall beare his judgment whosoever he be	And	He that faults us in absence for that which in presence he made shewe to approve shall by a double guilt of flattery and slaunder violate the Bands both of Friendship and Christianity.

Mary Farrar widdowe
Mother of this Family
And aged about Fourscore yeares

" That bidds adue to all Feares and hopes of this world and only desires to serve God.

" To the matter of this declaracion being in such generall Termes, I said I thought it without exception, but prayed leave to except against a circumstance, namely the Inscription, being the proper character of the Jesuits in every book and exhibit of theirs. He said it was that Auspitious name worthy to be Alpha and Omega of all our doings and we are commanded to write such things on the posts of our houses and uppon the gates.   I told him I was farr from excepting against the sacred and saving name of Jesus, only I would have it written at length or any other wayes to have differenced it from that the papists only use but not protestants.   And that the text he mencioned was in the Ould

Testament where there was no mencion of Jesus, but of Jehovah (to my remembrance). But we passed from this towards the Chappell (being about 40 paces from the house) yet staid a litle (as with a parenthesis) by a glass of sacke, sugar cake and a Fine napkin brought by a mannerlie Maide, which refresht my memorye to tell him what my Lord Bishop of Lincolne said of them, wherein yet I brake noe Lawes of humanity nor Hospitality though spoken at his table. For he said nothing but what they might and were glad to heare being but the Relacion of the Grave and discreet Answeres (as my lord himself termed them) of the ould gentlewoman to some of his Lordship's expostulacions.

" To that part Concerning the yonge Deacon whom his Lordship had heard of to come from Cambridge to officiate in their Chappell, He (innuendo even the yonger sonne who onlie was the speaker) said that himself was the yonge deacon intended, that he is two and forty yeares ould, was a Fellow of a house in Cambridge, and hath taken orders of deacon (to say nothing of his having beene at Rome whereof I could have excepted noe more against him than he might to me). For having beene soe long in labor of the Chappell it is now high tyme we were Churcht.

" At the entring whereof he made a lowe obeizance, fewe yards further a lower, coming to the halfe pace which was at the East end where the Table stood he bowed to the ground (if not prostrated himself); then went up into a Faire large reading place, a preaching place being of the same proportion right over against it. The Mother with all her Traine which were her daughters and daughters daughters had a Faire Iland seate.

" He placed me above uppon the halfe pace with two Faire long windowe Cushions of greene velvet before me; over against me were there such another seat, soe suited but noe bodie to sitt in it. The daughters four sonnes kneeled all the while on the edge of the halfe pace, all in black gownes. And they went to Church in Thrumbd * Monmouth Capps (as my Man said for I looked not back). The rest all in black, save one of the daughters

* " Thrum—a tuft, tassel or fringe of threads at the edge of a piece of cloth." *O.E.D.*
Peckard reads " round " instead of " Thrumbd ".

daughters who was in a Friers gray gowne. Wee being thus placed, the Deacon (for soe I must now call him) with a very loude and distinct voice beganne with the Lettanye and read divers prayers and Collects in the Book of Comon Prayer and Athanasius Creede, and Concluded with the Peace of God &c. All ended the Mother with all hir Company attended my Comeing downe. But hir Sonne Deacon told hir I would staye a while to veiwe the Chappell. Soe with all their civill Salutacions towards me which I returned them a Farr of and durst come noe neerer, least I should have light uppon one of the Virgins, not knowing whether they would have taken a kisse in good part or noe, they departed home.

" Now none but the deacon and I left, I observd the Chappell in generall to be Fairlie and sweetelie adorned with hearbes and flowers naturall in some places and Artificiall upon every pillar along both sides the Chappell, such as are in Cathedralls, with Tapers (I meane greate Virgin wax candles) on every pillar. The halfe pace at the upper end (for there was noe other division betwixt the Body of the Chappell and the East part) was all Covered with Tapestrye. And uppon that halfe pace stood the Communion Table (not Altar wise as was reported) with a Rich Carpet hanging very large uppon the halfe pace, and some plate as a Chalice and Candlestick with wax candles. By the Preaching place stood the Font, the legge, laver and Cover all of Brasse, cutt and Carved. The Cover had a Crosse erected; the Laver of the Bignes of a Barbers Bason. And this is all I had leasure to observe in the Chappell, save that I asked for the Organs, which he told me were not here but that they had a pair in their house. I also asked what use they made of soe many Tapers; he said to give them light when they could not see without them.

" Then, having formerlie (as I said before) obtained leave to say what I listed, I asked him to whom he made all those Curtesies: he said to God. I asked him if the papists make any other Answers for their bowing to Images and Crucifixes, yet we account them Idolaters for soe doeing. He said we have noe such warrant for the one, but for the other we had a Precept to do all things with decency and order as he took this to be; I demanded then why he used not the same solempnity in his service at his house and whether he thought that Chappell more holy than his house? He said noe, but that God was more immediatelie present whilst we were worshipping him in his Temple. I replied that I thought God was as present at Paules Crosse as in Paules Church, and at the Preaching place at White-hall and Spittle Sermons as els where, for wheresoever two or three are gathered together in his name God is in the midst of them. And yet in those places, noe not in the Bodie of the Church though there be a Sermon and prayers there, we do not use this Threefold Reverence, nor any lowe bowing unles in the Chauncell towards the East where an Altar or some Crucifix is. He answered me something of the Trinary number for his thrice bowing which I did not understand nor well heare.

" This (as all other our discourse) being ended with mildness and moderacion (on his part at least) I said further, Sith their devotions (from which they would be loath to be diverted or interrupted, as in their said protestacion may appeare) are more strict and regular than usuall, and if in their Consciences they were perswaded that all their formalities and Ceremonies were but Adiaphora (things indifferent) I then thought they were as wise as Serpents (in the Scripture sense) in Complying soe with Church Ceremonies that they might the safelier hold on their Course without Exception. For in this Compartment I thought Authoritie would not except against them unles for exceeding the Cathedralls who make but one Reverence, whereas they make three. Hee said I spake like one that (it seemed) have had experience in the world.

" Being now neere 12 a Clock we ended our discourse and I called for my Horses, hoping thereuppon that he would have invited me to stay dinner; not that I cared for his or any man's meate (for you had given me a dinner in soe good a breakfast), but that I might have gaigned more time to have seen and observed more of their fashions and whether the Virgins and yonger sort would have mingled with us, with divers other things that a dinner tyme would have best ministred matter for. But in sted of making me stay, he also helpt me in calling for my horses accompanying me even to my stirrup: and so I not returneing into the house, as we friendlie met we friendlie parted.

"Many more Questions I thought on when it was too late and yet you see I was not Idle for the short time I stayed. I asked him of their Monethly receiving of the Sacrament and whether their servants when they received were attended by the Masters and Mistresses and not suffered so much as to lay or take away their owne Trenchers (as I had heard); whereat he smiled as at a Frivolous Fable and said the only difference from other dayes was that the Servants that day that they received sate at the same Table with them.

"I heard also that they never roast any meate, onlie boyle and Bake, but not in past, that their Servants may not be so much hindered from their devotions. And that they have but one Horse among them all. But of these I made no mencion. They are extraordinarilie well reported of by their Neighbours, that they are very liberall to the poore, at great Cost in prepareing phisick and surgery for the sick and sore, whom they also visit often. And that some 60 or 80 poore people they task with Catechisticall Questions, which when they come and can make Answers, therunto they are rewarded with money and their dinner, by means of which Corodye of meate and money the poore Catecumens learne their lessons well and soe their bodies and soules are well fed.

"I find them full of humanity and humility, and others speak as much of their charity, which I also verilye believe, and therefore am farr from Censuring them of whom I thinke much better than of my selfe. My opposeing some of their opinions and practise (as you may see in this my Relacion, wherein I may have varied in some Circumstances, but nothing from the Substance) was only by way of Argument and for myne owne better Informacion. I shall be glad to observe how wiser men will Judge of them or imitate their Course of life.

"I intended not a Third part of this when I beganne (as you may see by my first lines). But one thing drawing on another I have now lefte out but little or nothing to my rememberance, saving what I thought fitt in good manners uppon my First

afront to make way for my welcome and ad captandam bene-volentiam (which is not worth the repeating if I could). And I am something better at acting such a part than at relateing it, though good at neither. After this longe and tedious relacion I must now make but short thankes to you and my Ladie for my longe and kind welcome, wherein my wife joynes with me, praying your remembering our loving respects to our kind Neeces, hopeing the good Schollers at Westminster are well. And soe I leave you all to the grace of God and am
The same your loving Friend and Servant."

This admirable letter was written within a few days of the events that it describes and might never have been heard of again. But some years later, in circumstances of which we know nothing, it, or a copy of it, fell into the hands of an enemy, someone who eagerly seized on it as a weapon which, if used with sufficient lack of scruple, could be turned to good propagandist effect against the Ferrars. A Puritan pamphleteer, highly skilled in the technique of a vile trade, was given the task of making all the use that he could of it; and the result was the publication of *The Arminian Nunnery*. It is interesting to set the two documents side by side and to let the comparison speak for itself.

Here, then, is the text of this notorious tract.*

The ARMINIAN NUNNERY
or
A BRIEF DESCRIPTION AND RELATION
of the late erected *Monasticall* Place, called
the ARMINIAN NUNNERY at little GIDDING
in HUNTINGTON-SHIRE

*Humbly recommended to the wise consideration
of this present* PARLIAMENT.

The Foundation is by a Company of FARRARS
at GIDDING †

Printed for *Thomas Underhill*, MDCXLI.

---

* From the copy in the library of Clare College, Cambridge.
† Below the title appeared a crudely executed wood-cut, showing a nun

" There stands a faire House well scituated with a fine Grove and sweet Walks, Letticed and Gardined on both sides; their livelihood or Revenew about 500 l. *per Annum*. One of my Lord *Mountagues* Mansion-Houses being within two or three miles off called *Hemmington House* not farre from *Oundle*.

" A Gentleman comming to visit the said House, was first brought to faire spacious Parlour, where soone after appeared the old Gentlewomans second sonne, a Batchelour of a plain presence, but pregnant of speech and parts, unto whom when I had deprecated and excused my selfe for so sudden and bold a visit, he entertained me with seeming civilitie and humilitie.

" After deprecations and some complements past betwixt us, he said I should see his Mother if I pleased, and I shewing my desire, hee went up into a Chamber and presently returned with his Mother, (a tall, ancient Gentlewoman about 80 yeares of age), shee being Matron of the *House*, his elder brother a Priest-like man in habit and haire. Now he had a Sister married in the *House* to one Mr Cooles (*sic*), who had 14 or 15 Children in the *House*, and of these with a man-servant and 2 or 3 maid-servants the *Family* then consisted.

" I was permitted to salute the Mother and Daughters, as we use to salute other women: and after we were all sitten Circular, I had leave to speak ingenuously of what I had heard and did or might conceive of their *House*. I first told him what I had heard of the Nunns at Gidding: of *two watching and praying all night*; of their *Canonicall houres*; of their *Crosses* on the outside and inside of the *Chappell*; of an *Altar* richly decked with *Tapestry*, *Plate* and *Tapers*; of their *Adorations, genuflections* and *geniculations*, which I told them plainly might strongly savour of Superstition and Popery.

" Now you must understand that the younger Brother who first came unto me is a jolly pragmaticall and Priest-like fellow, and is the mouth for all the rest, and he began to cut me off, and

---

with a rosary in her hand, and a small church in the background. Contrary to my earlier opinion, I think the drawing of the church is conventional and is not to be taken as an actual representation of Little Gidding at that time.

answered with a serious protestation (though not so properly) that he did as verily beleeve the Pope to be *Antichrist,* as any article of his Faith, which I noted and gave the hearing; and therein if he spake from his heart, he much differed from the opinions of Priest *Shelford,* Priest *Squire,* Dr. Drassig, the red Dragon of *Arminians,* and other eminent *Arminians.*

He denied the place to be a Nunnery, and that none of his Neeces were *Nunnes;* but hee confessed that two of his *Nieces* had lived the one thirtie, the other thirtie and two years Virgins, and so resolved to continue (as he hoped they would) to give themselves to *Fasting* and *Prayers;* but had made no *Vowes.*

" For their *Canonicall hours,* he said they usually prayed 6 times a day, viz. 2 times a day publikly in the *Chappell,* and 4 times a day more privately in the *House,* in the *Chappell* after the Order of the Booke of Common Prayer, at both times chanting out aloud the *Letany;* and in their *House* particular private Prayers for a *Familie.*

" And hee being asked, if they spent so much time in *Praying,* they would leave little for *preaching,* or for their weakly calling for which the *Text* is pregnant: *He that turneth away his eares, from hearing the Law, his Prayer is abominable:* Pro. 18 and 19. And the fourth *Commandment, Six dayes shalt thou labour &c.* Unto which this Priest-like pregnant Prolocutor answered but slubbingly, That sometimes a neighbour *parson* would come and preach in their *Chappell;* and to the other, That their Calling (forsooth) was *to serve God,* which he tooke to be best: Oh the stupid and blind devotion of these people, for Men and Women in health of able and active bodies and parts to have no particular *Callings,* or to quit their *Callings,* and betake themselves to I wot not what new forme of *Fasting* and *Prayer,* and a contemplative life, a lip-labour devotion, Eccl. 4 & 17 which by the word of God is no better than a specious kind of idlenesse, as *St Augustine* termes to be but *splendida peccata:* as if diligence in our particular lawfull callings were no part of our service to God.

" And doubtlesse such a Monastick Innovation in a settled Church-government is of dangerous consequence in many respects.

" For their *night-watching* and *rising at 4 of the Clock in the morning* (which was much for the Matron of 80 yeares of age, and her Grandchildren) the Priest-like Prolocutor did not want a premeditated excusive justification: But how neere it complieth with the superstitious *Nunneries* in Popish places beyond the Seas, I and others that have travelled and seene them may plainely perceive and notifie; especially considering hee could not but confesse there were every night two (alternatim) continued in their Devotions untill the rest rose.

" For their divers *Crosses,* the Prolocutor made me this answere; That they were not ashamed of the badge of Christian profession, which the first Propugnators of Faith bore in their Banners, and which are in our *Church Discipline* retained unto this day.

" How confused and absurd this Crosse Answere was, let every Christian man judge.

" On the Chimney-peice where wee sate, there was a Manuscript Tableture with this Inscription following, whereof I desired, and had a Coppy transcribed.

✠

I H S

He that by reproofe of our errors or remembrance of that which is more perfect seeks to make us better is welcome as an angel of God.	*and*	Hee that by a cheerful participation of that which is good confirms us in the same, is welcome as a Christian Friend.
	But	
He that any way goes about to divert or disturb us in that which is and ought to bee amongst Christians though it be not usuall with the world, is a burthen whiles he stayes and shall beare his judgement whosoever he be.	*and*	Hee that faults us in absence for that which in presence hee made shew to approve of, shall by a double guilt of flattery and slander violate the bonds of Friendship and Christianity.

" MARY FERRAR, Widdow, *Mother and Matron of this Familie ; aged about* 80 *yeares, that bids adue to all feares and hopes of this world, and desires to serve God.*

" The Letters of the top of which Inscription are the proper Characters of the Jesuites in every *Booke* and *Exhibite* of theirs. And the lines of the Inscription, how full of nonsense, justification and ostentation of superstitious devotion, besides their Creation of *Angels of* God; Let every understanding Christian Reader or hearer hereof judge.

" The Prolocutor in justification of the Jesuiticall *forme* of letters which I excepted against; he said it was the auspicious name worthy to be the *Alpha* and *Omega* of all our Actions, and wee are commanded *to write such things upon the posts of our Houses, and upon our Gates*: Whereas indeed the Text which hee arrived at is in the Old Testament and not in the New, where there is no mention of *Jesus* but Jehovah: And the words are most plainly, *Moses* Precept of the Law of God, and not of the Name, &c. *Deut.* 6.&c.

" Therefore this his Apologeticall answere was nothing but ignorant Eloquence, or eloquent ignorance; most grossly and absurdly applied.

" This Prolocutor confessed himselfe to bee about 42 yeares old, was a fellow in a House in *Cambridge* (he named not what *House*) and that he had taken Orders of a Deacon (but he said nothing of his having beene at *Rome*, as it is well knowne he hath beene.)

" Now I was invited by this Deacon to goe with him into the Chappell to their devotion, at the entrance whereof this Priest-like deft Deacon made a low obeysance, a few paces farther lower, and comming to the halfe-pace which is at the East end where the *altered Table* stood, hee bowed and prostrated himself to the ground; then he went up into a faire large reading place (having placed mee above with a faire large Window Cushion of green velvet before me). The *Mother Matron* with all her *Traine*, which were her *Daughters* and *Daughters Daughters*, who with four *Sonnes* kneeled all the while on the bodie of the halfe pace, all being in black gownes, and as they came to Church in round Monmouth Capps, all I say in blacke, save one of the Daughters who was in a Friers grey gowne.

" We being all placed before the Deacon (for now so we must call him) with a very loud and shrill voyce began and trolled out the *Letanie*, and read divers other Prayers and Collects in the Book of *Common Prayer* and *Athanasius* his Creed; and concluded with the forme of words, of, *The peace of God*, &c.

" This Service ended, the *Mother* with all her Company attending my comming downe; but I durst not come very neere lest I might happily have light upon one of the Virgins lippes, not knowing whether they would have taken a second kisse in good part or no, with their civil salutations towards mee, which I returned them a far off, they departed from the Chappell home.

" Now the Deacon and I left, I observed the Chappell in generall to bee fairely and speciously adorned with herbes and flowers naturall and artificiall, and upon every pillar along on both sides the Chappell (such as are in Cathedrall Churches) *Tapers*; I meane, great Virgin-waxe-Candles on every Pillar: The *halfe-pace* at the upper end (for there was no other division between the body of the Chappell and the East end) was all covered with Tapestry and upon that halfe-pace stood the *Altar-like Table*, with a rich Carpet hanging very large on the halfe-pace, and some Plate, as a Challice, and Candlesticks with waxe-candles in them: By the preaching place stood the Font, a Leg-laver and cover all of Brasse cut and carved with Imagery worke, the Laver of the bignesse of a Barbers Bason, and the Cover had a Crosse erected on it. And this is all I had leisure to observe in the Chappell.

" Then I made bold in temperate termes to aske the Deacons what use they made of so many *Tapers* on the Table, and in the Chappell, he answered (forsooth) to give them light, when they could not see without them. And having formerly as I said before obtained leave to say what I listed, I asked him to whom he made all these Courtesies, bowings and prostrations, he said to God; I told him the Papists make no other answere for their bowing to Images and Crucifixes, yet we account them Idolaters for so doing, as justly wee may: Hee said wee have no such warrant for the one; but for the other we had a precept (forsooth) *to doe all things with decencie and order*, as he tooke this to be. I demanded Then why hee used not the same solemnitie in his house, and whether he thought the Chappell more holy then his *House*, he said no, but that God was more immediately present in the *Chappell* then in the *House*, whilst we were worshipping him. I replied that God was as present at *Paules Crosse*, as in

Paules Church, at the Preaching-place at *Whitehall* and the *Spittle-Sermons*, as in other Churches and Chappells.   For *wheresoever two or three*, &c. and in those fore-named places, no not in the bodie of any Churches, though there be Sermons and Prayers there, we do not use this threefold reverence, or bowing or pros-trating, no nor the Papists themselves, unlesse in the Chancell towards the East, wherein an Altar or some Crucifix is; He answered me somewhat confusedly, for this their *trinary number* of bowing which I did not well understand, nor well conceive what he meant.

"It seemes moreover that at their monthly receiving the Sacrament (which this defendant Deacon performeth and conse-crateth the *bread* and *wine*) their servants when they received, were attended by their Master and Mistris, and not suffered to lay or take away their owne trenchers as it is reported.

"They also take upon them to be Phisitians and Chirurgions in ministring Physicke and Chirurgery for the sick and sore, and pretend to be very charitable to the poore; but as it is verily thought in a meritorious way.

"They also take upon them to be Catechisers and to task many poore people with Catechisticall questions; which when they come and can make answere thereunto, they are rewarded with money and their dinners and so they pretend they feed the poores bodies and soules, But their Catechisme or Catechisticall questions (some say) are strange ones and and far different from our Orthodox Catechismes.   You may take notice that since the observation of the premisses, th'old Matron of the place is dead.

"And now beloved and Christian Reader, you have had an ingenuous Relation of this late erected *religious house* for the ser-vice of God (as the Founders would have it termed and held.) But certes we may wonder at nothing more that a settled Church-government our Bishops who are accounted *Governours of the Church* will permit any such erection or Foundation, so nearly complying with *Popery*, and that by a fond and fantasticall *Family of Farrars*, the principall Priest a *poly-pragmaticall* Fel-low, having beene at *Rome*, and there (as it is credibly reported) he was conformable to all the abominable *Ceremonies* and *Services* of the *Church of Rome*. Now forsooth, in outward shew, hee would pretend that hee and the rest disclaime the *Pope* and *Poperie*, but by and by you shall see him and his Companions crouching, cringing, and prostrating to the ground to the Altar-like poore *Communion-Table*, or the rich gilded candlesticks, and waxe Tapers and other knacks thereon standing; And for another shew that they would not be accounted Popish, they have gotten the *Booke of Martyrs* in the Chappell; but few or none are suffered to read therein, but onely it is there (I say) kept for a shew; and besides their lip-labour of trolling out the *Letanie* foure times a day, they have promiscuous private prayers all the night long by nightly turnes, just like as the English *Nunnes* at Saint *Omers* and other Popish places; which private prayers are (as it seemes) taken out of *John Cozens* his *Cozening Devotions* (as they are rightly discovered to be by Orthodox men) and extracted out of divers Popish *Prayer-Bookes*. This *Fryer like Familie*, and as they are not unfitly termed *Arminian Nunnery* have divers other Commick and Mimmick actions of will-worship to the great dishonour of Almighty God, who will be served *in spirit and truth* and he will once say unto them as hee did by the prophet Isaiah, to the superstitious and ceremonious *Jewes*, *Who hath required this at your hands? &c.*

" *W. Cant.** Surely we may marvell that the present *Primate* of *All England and Metropolitane* being the principall *Governour* of the *Church*, under his sacred *Majestie*, and as hee professeth such an *Anti-Papist* and enemy to superstition and *Idolatry*, should permit this *Innovation*, and connive at such *canting* betwixt the barke and the tree in matter of Religion: But by what hath been related of these Peoples practises, we see that position made good, That *Arminianisme* is a bridge to *Popery*, the bridge was not onely made (a great part of the Clergie of this Land being downright *Arminians*) but some have past over it; witnesse Priest *Shelford*, Priest *Cozens*, and This Familie in this Booke treated on with divers others, and had not God of his mercy undermin'd the Chiefe Arches of that bridge, causing them to fall in the River of confusion, wee have cause to thinke that the

* i.e. Archbishop Laud.

greater part of this Land would also have followed the rest; but now God hath hindred it, not only by breaking the bridge in the just downfall of many of the chiefe of the *Arminian Faction*, but also by setting up that strong, high, and thick wall of the late Parliamentary nationall Protestation which (as also for all his mercies at all times, especially for this years wonders) his name be for ever praised (say I) and let all Protestants say, *Amen.*
Finis."

The pamphlet is clearly unworthy of critical examination; it is interesting only as a sample of sectarian propaganda of the period and as an indication of the feverish heat to which opinion had been roused.   John Ferrar said all that need be said about it when he described it as being " stuffed with abominable false-hoods and such stories as the devil himself would be ashamed to utter ".

Its publication naturally threw John into great disturbance of mind and he wrote at once to Lenton.   The lawyer replied promptly.   He acknowledged that this " libellous pamphlet " was clearly based on the letter that he had written to Sir Thomas Hetley some seven years previously; but how the letter had come to fall into the hands of " such hucksters " he had no idea. He had known nothing of the pamphlet before its publication; it was, he protested, a monstrous travesty of what he had written and he expressed his disgust at the lies and slanders contained in it.

John gladly accepted Lenton's explanation, but he knew very well that the publication of the libellous screed was a true measure of the implacable malice of his enemies.   It was a direct threat of the most serious nature.   Copies of *The Arminian Nunnery* were thrust into the hands of Members of Parliament as they went to the House and were distributed in large numbers amongst the newly raised Parliamentary levies.   It came to John Ferrar's knowledge that a company of troops recently recruited in Essex, who were under orders to move to the north of England, had been served out with copies of the pamphlet and that attempts were made to divert them in their northward march for an assault

upon Little Gidding, " but God Almighty in His special providence did turn away their fury at that time and it then passed
over ".

In October 1641 came the news of Williams's appointment to
the Archbishopric of York.   A month later the Grand Remon-
strance was adopted in Parliament.   Just before the end of the
year there were riots outside the House of Lords; Williams was
hustled by a hostile crowd and had his gown torn off his back.
A week afterwards came the attempted impeachment of the five
members.   The *tempo* of events was quickening and it was now
inexorably clear that England stood on the eve of civil war.   On
23 February 1642 the Queen, taking the Crown Jewels with her,
sailed from Dover; and the King, after a tender farewell, galloped along the cliffs to follow the course of the vessel till it was
out of sight.   He returned to Greenwich with his plans finally
made.   His intention was to go north at once, where he knew he
could count on solid loyalty, and to occupy either Hull or New-
castle, so as to keep open his communications with the Continent.

E

IV

ON 9 March the King, accompanied by Prince Rupert and Prince Charles, was at Newmarket, where a Parliamentary deputation waited on him to present a statement of grievances. Charles refused any compromise; he now knew beyond doubt that Parliament was determined to usurp his authority and destroy the Church. He remained only a day or two in Newmarket and, moving northward by easy stages, he rode into York on the 19th.

The exact stages of the journey are not clear. It may have been on the 12th or 13th that the royal party passed through Huntingdon, where the King conferred a knighthood upon the high sheriff of the county. John Ferrar says that they spent a night in Huntingdon; but in view of what was to follow, it would seem more likely that their stopping-place was some miles farther west, perhaps Kimbolton. For on the following day, moving northward to reach Stamford that night, they were travelling on the road that comes up through Winwick; and it is difficult to see why they should have taken this route if they had been travelling from Huntingdon.

This March day in 1642 was to be one of the most memorable in the annals of Little Gidding. For as the King was approaching Winwick, he looked eastward towards the low range of hills, and enquired of his equerry what house that was that stood so pleasantly. He was told that it was the manor-house of Little Gidding. " Is it that? " commented Charles. " I must go and visit it. Doth not our way lie beneath it? " Meanwhile it would seem that the royal party had been espied afar off from the windows of the house. One can imagine the excitement of the household. They set out forthwith down the hill to the bridge over the Alconbury Brook to attend the King's coming, " as most desirous to see him and to kiss his hands ".

" So the King approaching foremost of all, they went all to

meet him and kneeling down prayed God to bless and preserve his majesty and keep him safe from his enemies' malice."

Charles gave them his hand to kiss, and at that moment Prince Rupert galloped up and made the laughing suggestion that, to save the ladies the labour of climbing the hill homeward, they should take them on horseback. The ladies excused themselves and asked leave to lead the way on foot; and so, after an interval of nine years, the King came again to Little Gidding and John Ferrar made haste to receive him.

They went first into the church, which Charles was pleased to admire. Turning to one of his gentlemen, he enquired where were all the images in the church, of which there had been so much talk. " I see none."

" Sir," he was answered, " you see all that ever were in this place."

The King smiled.

" I knew it full well ", he said, " that there never were any. What will not malice and slander invent ? "

When they had seen all that could be shown them in the church, they repaired to the house, and the King at once asked where was the great book that was being made for Prince Charles. This was the volume, an arrangement of the Pentateuch according to its subject matter, which had been planned in the lifetime of the younger Nicholas; and now the enormous book, magnificently bound in purple velvet, was brought in and the Duke of Richmond observed that one of the King's strongest guardsmen would be needed to carry it. It was laid on the table before the King and, with the two Princes standing by him, he began to turn the pages, noting and commenting on the skill of its compilation and the aptness of its many illustrations.

" Charles," he said, " here's a stately book indeed."

And for two hours he continued his perusal, asking many questions, taking notice of many points of detail, praising the beauty of the binding, and remarking that many years' work must have gone to its preparation. Prince Rupert joined his admiration to the King's.

" Sir," he declared to his cousin, " your father hath the goodliest, greatest ship in the world, but you will have the gallantest, glorious, largest book and such as the world cannot compare with it.   For I never saw such paper before and believe there is no book of this largeness to be seen in Christendom."

At last the King closed the book and Prince Charles asked if he might not now take it for his own.   But it was explained by one of the family that it was not yet finished as to the binding and decoration; this would be completed with the least delay.

" Well," said the King, " you must content yourself for a while."

" The gallantest, glorious, largest book "; it is not a bad description of this most remarkable volume.   John Ferrar, writing towards the end of his life, probably in 1653, speaks of it as being then still at Gidding; it seems certain that it was never actually presented to the Prince.   Its weight and size make it quite difficult for one man to carry comfortably; for it measures 2 feet 5 inches by 1 foot 8 inches and has nearly 450 pages of very heavy paper, each sheet having the text and various engravings pasted on.   It contains an elaborate arrangement of " the whole law of God as it is delivered in the five Books of Moses ", set under three headings—moral, ceremonial, and political, each of these sections being further sub-divided.   There follows a harmony of Old Testament types and prophecies related to their fulfilment in the Gospels.   Then comes a " Discourse of the estate of the Jews " from a writing by Dr Thomas Jackson, lengthy extracts from a work entitled *Moses Unveiled*, and a miscellany of other matter.

The history of the volume is obscure.   After John Ferrar's death nothing is known about it until its purchase in 1776 by a clergyman named Bourdillon.   This is recorded in the book itself. About the beginning of the nineteenth century it was quite unexpectedly discovered in a walled-up cupboard in a house at Brookmans Park, near Hatfield, belonging to the Gaussen family. It remained in that family's possession until a few years ago, when it was acquired by the Victoria and Albert Museum, its present resting-place.

After his inspection of the book, the King was taken to see

the rooms where the poor widows maintained by the family lived. These rooms were laid out after the manner of the Dutch alms houses and the King was much impressed by their cleanliness and pleasant aspect.   He spoke for some time with the inmates. Then, going out into the garden, as he was walking down a long arbour, he took five pieces of gold from his pocket and handed them to the Duke of Richmond.

" Let these be given to the poor widows," he said.   " It is all I have, else they should have more; and will them to pray for me."

He commented again upon the fine situation of the house upon its little hill; and then he was interrupted by some of his young equerries who had been foraging indoors and now emerged from the buttery with apple-pies and cheese-cakes, which they merrily offered to the Prince.

" Sir, will your highness taste?   It is as good an apple-pie as ever we eat."

Wine was served in the house, and soon the King declared that it was growing late and they must be on their way.   The horses were brought to the door; as the King mounted, all the household knelt and prayed for his safety and that God would give him a long and happy reign.   To which he answered, " Pray for my speedy and safe return again "; and so they took the road for Stamford and were gone.

For those at Little Gidding it had been a day never to be forgotten, a joyous interlude in the midst of many trials.   Yet, as John Ferrar thought over the events of the day that evening, the profound significance of the King's northward journey must have been clearly apparent to him.   The die was now cast; this was the first move in a campaign, the preliminary to the final and now irrevocable trial of strength between King and Parliament. Within a few days of leaving Little Gidding Charles was in York with the intention of securing the port of Hull.   On 22 April Prince Rupert and Prince James were received and entertained in the town; but when the King with an escort of three hundred cavalrymen approached on the following day, the governor of the fortress raised the drawbridges and refused admission.   After some futile parleying and the formal proclamation of the governor as a traitor, the King withdrew to York.   The chance to save Hull for the Royalist cause was lost.

Rather more than a month later, on 2 June, Parliament dispatched to the King a series of demands so insolent and provocative as to constitute a virtual ultimatum.   Charles recognized this as clearly as anyone, though he still cherished the desperate hope of a peaceful settlement.   But events were now moving inexorably to a climax.   On the Parliamentary side mobilization was already well advanced.   Large numbers of Royalist supporters were rallying to York and from many parts of the country came professions of loyalty and offers of help in men, money, and materials.

Royalist sympathy was strong in both ancient universities. During August the Oxford and Cambridge colleges were raising funds and assembling much of their gold and silver plate as gifts to the King's cause.   In Cambridge elaborate plans were made for conveying the treasure, to a total estimated value of between £8,000 and £10,000, to the Royalist headquarters, now moved to Nottingham.

" This ", wrote Dr Peter Barwick in his memoir of his brother, who was at that time a fellow of St John's College, " could not be effected without first outwitting Cromwell who had been apprized of their design by some of the Townsmen of Cambridge (by whose interest he had been chosen a Member of Parliament for that town) and with a disorderly band of peasants on foot, lay in wait for the rich booty at a place called Lowler Hedges, between Cambridge and Huntingdon.*   But Mr. Barwick and some other select persons of the university, to whose care and prudence the management of this important affair was committed, having got intelligence of Cromwell's way-laying them, sent away the royal supply through by-roads, convoyed by a small party of horse, that very night in which Cromwell with his foot beset the common road, or else the spoil had the next morning certainly fallen into the enemy's hands.   He that was made choice of to conduct this expedition was the Rev. Mr. Barnabas Oley, a man of great

* Near the village of Lolworth.

prudence and very well acquainted with all the by-ways through which they were to pass.   He was president of Clare Hall. . . . Under the protection of God's good providence he arrived safe at Nottingham where he had the honour to lay at his Majesty's feet this small testimony and earnest of the university loyalty at that very time when the royal standard was set up in the castle there." *

We can date the expedition quite precisely, for it was on 22 August that Charles raised his standard at Nottingham.   We also know that some of the plate sent from Cambridge was in fact intercepted by Parliament men and never reached the King; this seems to have been in a separate convoy.   What is made clear in a statement printed by John Ferrar's son some sixty years later is that his father had been an active collaborator in the enterprise and had no doubt worked in close touch with Oley, who was an old friend of the family's.†   The statement, of which a copy is preserved at Magdalene College, includes the following words:

" Mr. Ferrar [i.e. John Ferrar's son] and his father were great sufferers for their loyalty to King Charles the First, having their estate sequestered and being forced to fly out of the land, particularly for assisting in conveying to his Majesty the Cambridge University plate which was presented by the University for the relief of that good King."

We know nothing of the exact part played by John Ferrar; but it is a tempting and not unreasonable speculation that Barnabas

---

* *The Life of the Rev. Dr. John Barwick, D.D. etc., written in Latin by his Brother Dr. Peter Barwick; translated into English by Hilkiah Bedford* (London, 1724), pp. 23 ff.   John Barwick became Dean of St Paul's after the Restoration.

† Barnabas Oley was a Clare man who took his B.A. in 1621 and became a fellow of the college in 1627.   Later he held the offices of tutor and president, and was largely responsible for the building of the present Old Court. He was vicar of Great Gransden near St Neot's, from 1633 till his death in 1686.   He was ejected from his fellowship and living in 1644, and suffered great hardship in the ensuing years.   To the first edition of Herbert's *Country Parson*, which was published in 1652, he prefixed a memoir of Herbert which includes a warm and moving tribute to Nicholas Ferrar with a short account of his life.

Oley's convoy, travelling by lanes and by-roads, may have passed through Little Gidding and perhaps made a stop there on its way. In any case, we can be sure that John did everything in his power to assist the enterprise and that he would have counted it an honour to be able to do so.

With the outbreak of hostilities we come to a period in the story of Little Gidding about which we have little knowledge. From this time onwards it becomes impossible to follow the fortunes of the family in any detail; we have only a few scattered and scanty allusions to what happened to them. One thing is clear. John Ferrar knew that, in the eyes of the Parliamentary leaders, he was a marked man; and as regional loyalties took clearer shape and the military campaign developed, he realized that, in remaining at Gidding, his position and that of his family was one of the utmost peril. We know nothing of the circumstances, later referred to by his son, in which the Little Gidding estate was sequestered. All that can be said for certain is that the time came when John decided that his only course was to leave Gidding and seek safety overseas. Years later, when he was an old and tired man, John wrote a letter to his son, urging him, when his time came to succeed to the estate, to continue that monthly thanksgiving which " was practised by your pious grandmother and devout uncle, the founders of our family ", and reciting some of the perils from which by God's merciful providence the family had been preserved.

" We were fain ", he says, " to submit to a long sequestration, for then the waves raged horribly. But that was not all: to save our consciences from what was imposed that that might not ruin also, we rather resolved to leave our native country and so I took you [and] my V.F. * and went beyond seas, and some of our dearest friends, fellows in our misery, did accompany us beyond the sea." †

Continuing, he records his thankfulness to God for their ultimate safe return to Gidding ; but he makes no reference to the duration of their exile nor to where it had been spent. This is

* His daughter Virginia Ferrar.
† Magdalene College MSS; John Ferrar to his son, n.d.

understandable, for he and his son had been together all the time and anyhow such matters were best not set down in writing. There is a letter from Leyden by Richard Crashaw after his ejection from Peterhouse in 1643-4, and this reveals the fact that Mary Collett, "the gentlest, kindest, most tender-hearted and liberal-handed soul I think this day alive", was also at Leyden at the time.* It is a fair assumption that members of the family were with her.

This seems to be the only evidence that we have, apart from one or two vague traditions which might suggest a sojourn in France. All we can say with assurance is that the family were compelled to seek refuge overseas and that they were away from Gidding for what may have been a matter of a few months, but was more probably a period of two years or longer. Meanwhile, young Ferrar Collett had been expelled from his fellowship at Peterhouse; as a colleague wrote to him on 28 June 1643, "these be very thundering times".† Other friends shared the same adversity; Barnabas Oley was amongst those evicted from Clare Hall, and Robert Mapletoft from Pembroke.

Those familiar with the earlier Little Gidding story will remember Robert's name. He was one of the family's most intimate and dearest friends ; he was also a relation by marriage, for his elder brother Joshua had married Susanna Collett. He and Nicholas Ferrar had loved one another most affectionately, and Little Gidding had been like a second home to him. When Nicholas died in 1637, it was Robert who had had the great and solemn privilege of conducting the office of burial and preaching the funeral sermon. We can share John Ferrar's wish that the text of the address had been preserved.

Early in 1644 Robert was ejected from his fellowship on his refusal to sign the covenant; he moved about from place to place and eventually, along with Peter Gunning, later Bishop of Ely and other Anglican clergy, he found shelter with Sir Robert

---

* See E. Crwys Sharland, "Richard Crashaw and Mary Collett" (*Church Quarterly Review*, January 1912, pp. 358 ff.), where the letter is given in full.

† Magdalene College MSS; P. Maxwell to Ferrar Collett.

Shirley of Staunton Harold in Leicestershire.* This young nobleman, who is still honourably known to his descendants as "Good Sir Robert", was a devout Churchman and zealous Royalist. During the tragic years of the civil war he made Staunton Harold a home for a number of evicted priests of the Church of England and twice suffered imprisonment for his loyalty. His finest monument is the church at Staunton Harold. Begun in 1652, it is one of the very few churches built in England during the Commonwealth. It stands on the site of an old chapel, which had by that time fallen into ruin, and is a magnificent fabric in the late Gothic manner. Sir Robert died in captivity in the Tower of London in 1656; his body was brought from London and lies in a vault beneath the chancel. Above the west door is a tablet with the following inscription, surely one of the finest epitaphs ever written:

In the yeare 1653
when all thinges Sacred were throughout ye nation
Either demolisht or profaned
Sir Robert Shirley, Barronet,
Founded this church;
Whose singular praise it is
to have done ye best thinges in ye worst times
And
hoped them in ye most callamitous.
Ye righteous shall be had in everlasting remembrance.

It has always been believed that Sir Robert's Bible, which is preserved in his family, was bound at Little Gidding and that the altar cloth, pulpit hangings, and other ornaments in the church were made there, too. The tradition has been firmly held for three hundred years, though no evidence was known to support it. It would seem that Robert Mapletoft's presence at Staunton Harold during those troubled years provides an intimate link with Little Gidding and suggests strong reason for

* J. Bentham, *History and Antiquities of Ely* (London, 1771), p. 235; E. P. Shirley, *Stemmata Shirleiana* (London, 1873), p. 152; Wood (ed. Bliss), *Fasti*, ii, 313; Echard, *Hist.* iii, 437.

believing the tradition to be true. For it is an attractive and natural supposition that the Bible may have been a gift to Sir Robert, a mark of personal affection and gratitude, and that the ornaments for the church were made at Little Gidding at Robert Mapletoft's suggestion. The family had much cause to be grateful to Shirley and would have rejoiced to be able to help in adorning the new church.

It is impossible to say when John Ferrar and his family returned to Little Gidding; we know that they must have been back, at the latest, by the early spring of 1645–6. It was by that time clearly apparent that the royalist cause was irretrievably lost and for that reason John may well have felt that, whatever the hazards, it was his duty to return home. He must have been thankful for the rest of his life that he had done so; for, in circumstances of high drama, he was to be allowed once more to show his loyalty to his sovereign by receiving and entertaining him at Gidding.

On 27 April 1646 three men rode out of Oxford. One was Sir John Ashburnham, treasurer and paymaster of the Royal army, the King's most faithful cavalier; the second was the Reverend Michael Hudson, most trusted of the Royal chaplains; the third, carefully disguised to pass as Ashburnham's servant, was the King himself. It was the beginning of that last desperate attempt to save the Royalist cause by an appeal to the Scots; on a longer perspective it was, for the King, the first step on that *via dolorosa* which was to end three years later on the scaffold in Whitehall.

The little party left Oxford at three o'clock in the morning and took the bold course of striking straight out on the London road. The bluff was successful and they had no difficulty in getting past the various patrols whom they encountered. They went through Dorchester, Henley, and Maidenhead, and then struck north-east towards Harrow. On the 28th they rested at Wheathamsted, near St Albans, and from thence they reached a village near Newmarket, where they lodged at the inn. The following night's journey brought them to Downham Market. At this point they decided to double back westward; and so it came about that on 1 May, most secretly and in the dead of night, the King came once more to Little Gidding and John Ferrar most dutifully received him.   The King and his companions had travelled more than two hundred miles since they had left Oxford and they must have been desperately tired.   Even so, John Ferrar, knowing the local circumstances and the ubiquity of Parliamentary agents in the neighbourhood, was emphatic that the King ought not to remain at Gidding during the coming hours of daylight; and after he had refreshed them he set out with the royal party and led them to a private house at the nearby village of Coppingford, where he knew they would be safe.   Here the King slept and went on the following night to Stamford.   On 5 May he reached the Scottish army headquarters at Newark.

Thus, as Peckard finely says, Little Gidding " was the very last place where this most unfortunate Prince was in the hands of those whom he might safely trust and under the protection of an honest and confidential friend ". *

For this final act of loyalty John Ferrar was to suffer a savage retribution.   Three or four months later, in July or August 1646, Little Gidding was raided by Parliamentary troops.   John had warning beforehand, and, for the protection of his family, got away from the house before the assault.   The soldiers ransacked both the church and house, tore down the organ at the west end of the church, lit a huge fire with the wreckage and roasted some sheep which they had killed in the pastures.   Then, as legitimate loot, they seized all the plate, furniture, and provisions that they could carry off and made away at their leisure.

We have no means of knowing what damage was actually done.   It cannot have been serious enough to render the house uninhabitable or the church unusable.   Probably there was a good deal of malicious violence inside the house and a serious search for incriminating papers; we are told that letters and other papers were burnt, including some of Nicholas Ferrar's original writings.   Whatever was done to the church organ, it was probably not damaged beyond repair; for some years later a friend of the family's, John Castell—he was a barrister and a

* *Memoirs of the Life of Mr. Nicholas Ferrar* (London, 1790), pp. 232–3.

son of the rector of Glatton—was writing as follows to John Ferrar:

" I hear that you have an organ which is somewhat defaced and if you do not intend to renew it and make it useful for yourself, if you will part with it, I can help you to a chapman for it; if you please to part with it, this gentleman, Mr. Watson your neighbour, if he may see it, will tell you whether it will be made useful for the future and what it is worth." *

The fabric of the church, particularly at the west end, must have been a good deal knocked about. The restoration of 1704 was a very thorough one. The west front had to be completely rebuilt and the church was shortened by about eight feet in the process.

* Magdalene College MSS; John Castell to John Ferrar, 27 February 1655.

V

OVER the next three years we have very little information about the course of events at Little Gidding. The household was by now quite a small one. John Ferrar and his wife, their son John and their daughter Virginia, Mr and Mrs Collett and Mary were still there; hardly any one of the others can have been left at home. The Collett daughters, apart from Mary, who had long been vowed to a single life, had married. Two of them were still living close at hand; for Judith had married the Reverend Solomon Mapletoft, a younger brother of Joshua and Robert, who was instituted vicar of Sawtry in March 1646-7. Joyce's husband was the Reverend Edward Wallis, who became rector of Little Gidding early in the following year.

All through the summer and autumn of 1647 the fate both of King and kingdom hung in the balance. Fairfax's headquarters were at Newmarket and thither the King had been escorted in June; it was not until the end of November that the grilles of " Carisbrooke's narrow cage " closed upon him. Troop movements of one kind and another were frequent in East Anglia; and when soldiers were billeted at Little Gidding the family could not have expected sympathetic treatment from them.

" We are very well and in quiet and no soldiers near us ", writes Virginia Ferrar to her mother; " I bless God we are in quiet and no soldiers near to molest us ", she reports to Anna Mapletoft. Some months later Mary Collett is writing to John Ferrar, who was evidently away from Gidding at the time.

" We had a regiment of horse come on Friday to quarter in our parts, they say but 3 or 4 days, and 4 is fallen to our lot, but with exceeding much ado not quartered in the house." *

Through all this time when all the tribulations foretold by Nicholas Ferrar seemed to be moving to their fulfilment, we may

* Magdalene College MSS; Virginia Ferrar to her mother, 20 June 1647; to Anna Mapletoft, n.d.; Mary Collett to John Ferrar, 12 December 1647.

believe that the quiet routine of the family's devotional life was maintained without interruption. Old friendships were not forgotten. Richard Drake, who had been a disciple of Lancelot Andrewes and had known the Ferrars for many years, sends a copy of the Bishop's *Preces Privatae*, newly translated from the Greek and published by himself.

" Sir," he writes to John Ferrar, " your acceptation of the Bishop's Devotions puts me in very good hopes that my intentions in the publishing of them will obtain the ends for which I made them speak English: viz., the commendation of his precious memory to posterity, the righting of his due reputation invaded by a spurious copy, and the advancement of devotion and piety, besides a special design of obtaining the intercession of pious souls for the unworthy translator. Among others I find to my comfort that I have gained yours, which I have the greater reason to rejoice in, as being confident that the ancient devotion of your worthy family [will] find a way to heaven, notwithstanding all the noise and distractions of the world. The great decline of Christianity which our eyes have seen with tears, should make the stronger union and association of souls; it is the only stock I know of that can be free from plunder, and if after all these storms we can but keep our souls, we shall, notwithstanding all our losses, be gainers in the end." *

It is finely said, and he goes on to speak of the King's passionate desire for peace and prays that God may yet bring a happy issue. But, humanly speaking, all hope of such a thing had long disappeared. For Royalists the unspeakable climax, when it came, was the final consummation of the long tragedy. All was now lost; and one of the immediate sequels to the setting-up of the Commonwealth was a new tide of Royalist emigration from a homeland that seemed doomed and stricken beyond redemption. John Ferrar was now in his seventieth year; but even he, with his long associations with the colony of Virginia, may well have considered going overseas to end his days. For the younger folk, with their lives before them and with looser ties at home, the

* Magdalene College MSS; Richard Drake to John Ferrar, S. Luke 1648.

call was clear and insistent. Mary Mapletoft, now married to a Mr Laurence Ward, left England for Virginia in the autumn of 1649; three of her cousins, the brothers John, Richard, and James Collett, went overseas early in 1650.

Mary Mapletoft was John Ferrar's grand-niece. Her parents were the Reverend Joshua Mapletoft, who had been vicar of Margaretting in Essex till his death in 1635, and Susanna, daughter of Mr and Mrs Collett. She had been entirely brought up at Little Gidding, and was always known in the family as " Mall ". She and Virginia Ferrar were contemporaries and inseparable companions, and a few of the letters that passed between them over a period of years are preserved in the Magdalene collection. She was now in her twenty-first year.

During the months preceding Mary's sailing for Virginia, the exact date of which cannot be determined, her mother wrote a couple of letters, one to Virginia Ferrar and one to John Ferrar, which provide some information about the circumstances under which emigrants were leaving the country and the feelings of those who were left at home.

" Miss Jonson on Saturday came to see us ", she tells Virginia, " Mall gave her the 2 books from you as your father sent up; she gives you many thanks for them and says she will give her husband one of them from you. She goes in the ' John and Catrine ' with Mr. Hill. I perceive she has to deal with a wary man. He takes all she has into his possession and promises her she shall have all accommodation the ship can afford to any, and bids her take care for nothing. . . . Next week she makes account to go a-shipboard to Gravesend, but knoweth not the day ".*

The second letter is addressed to John Ferrar. After saying that she is sending a bottle of syrup for Virginia, who was unwell, and giving directions for its use, she proceeds:

" On Friday I went into London to send letters to my children and to enquire for more cotton seeds, but could hear of none yet: this is the 10th letter I have sent after my dear friends since they

* Magdalene College MSS; Susanna Chedley to Virginia Ferrar, 7 August 1649.

went. The ships lie now but for a wind; 4 of them as I am told, and abundance of quality go in them.

"As I went, I met Mrs. Hard. Her husband went in the ship with Miss Jonson, for he is so in debt that he went away very secretly and, as she told me, the ship was searched for him too. She said he hath ventured £4000 to Virginia and hath had bad luck with his factors, they living most gallantly there and sending him little return in comparison; for he hath sent 40 men at a time and hath traded thither ever since you did, 26 years, as she saith.

"She told me she and her daughter, for she hath but one, went with her husband to Gravesend. And there she met with Miss Jonson, and she bewailed herself very much and told her Mr. Hill had dealt most unworthily with her when she came aboard, and put her into the gunroom, yet bound her and her maid and all she had over to him. I am very sorry for her, poor woman. . . .

"Do you not think they are there by this time? I hope they are. No more is heard of them, nor of the ships that went after them.

"I heard last week that one Mr. Simons his son, that went in those ships that Captain Bullock went in, is dead. He was a young gentleman of my dear son's acquaintance, of the same college, and his father lives not far from Mr. Bendish. His father's elder son and he ventured £300 with him. He died at the Downs of the small-pox; God's will must be done.*

"You hear, Sir, how all things go here. Lord, look down from heaven upon this miserable land! I meet with none now almost but tell me of some one going, and many are resolved to go, to Virginia. But if it were in my power I would order that the ship should be made to make more and better provision for the poor passengers and not fill their ships so full. (*sic*) . . . Truly, so men can get money, they make no matter of the lives of others. Those ships were mightily pestered and I hear 30 died out of that ship besides this gentleman."

She continues with a few more comments and then adds in a postscript:

* Edward Simons had been up at Trinity College, Cambridge, with her son, John Mapletoft.

F

" Old Sir Thomas Alesbury and all his family are gone out of this miserable land, either to France or Holland, I know not which, and have sold all that belonged to them. They went secretly away."

The letter throws a clear enough light on the character of the emigration. Those who were sailing for Virginia were Royalists who had decided on religious, political, moral, or other grounds that England was no fit place for them to remain in. The colony had always been strongly Royalist in sympathy and one of the Virginian Assembly's first actions after the execution of Charles I had been to denounce the Parliamentary leaders as traitors, to refuse recognition of the Commonwealth and to proclaim Charles II as the legitimate sovereign. This defiant action could not be ignored in London. A Parliamentary ordinance in October 1650 deprived the Virginian colony of all rights of free trade, ordering that none of their commodities were to be sold in any independent markets. The measure was followed twelve months later by the first of the celebrated Navigation Acts. Herein it was laid down that all goods grown or manufactured in Asia, Africa, or America should be accepted at English ports only if they had been transported in British ships, and that all products coming into England from whatever part of the world should be shipped direct from the place of their origin. The Act was aimed primarily at the Dutch, who for years had been transporting large quantities of Virginian tobacco at cheaper freightage rates than British shipmasters could afford, or were prepared, to offer. It also had, as it was intended to have, severely dislocating effects on the economy of Virginia, and the colonists were in no position to resist.

It can be assumed that during the civil war John Ferrar's correspondence with his friends in Virginia was much curtailed, if not completely interrupted. But once he was back at Gidding, he was soon actively concerning himself with the colony's affairs and it is from this period that we can see Virginia Ferrar beginning to emerge as a real figure in the development of the Virginian silk industry.

John Ferrar's accounts for the year 1649 show that during that period he sent out no fewer than 197 books to various settlers. There were Bibles, collections of sermons, copies of Herbert's poems, of Bishop Andrewes's *Devotions* and other spiritual works. The recipients were asked " to make return in any commodity they can and of tobacco to take as little as may be if other commodities are to be had ". The Ferrars had no use for tobacco on principle; it is more than once referred to with the strongest disapproval in the annals of the Little Academy, a " vile, stinking weed " which stupefied the faculties and made its addicts obnoxious to their fellow-men. But John was also sure—and his belief was shared by many of the Virginian pioneers—that the colonists' obsession with tobacco was bound to prove disastrous in the long run, since its cultivation could be increased only at the expense of the staple products. His view was sound and farsighted, and it is to be observed that a good deal of the economic legislation of the Virginian Assembly was directed to limiting the constantly increasing tobacco plantations. It is also a fact that none of the attempted checks proved effective; the market was still too good and profits too easy.

Only a small part of Virginia Ferrar's correspondence with her colonial friends has been preserved. Some of the letters are of real interest; the following admirable and racy epistle may be quoted as a sample:

" Excellent gentlewoman, Virginia is bound to you for your wishes and beseeches you to forgive her that she produces nothing worth your taking unless you be a tobacconist. But 'tis not her fault she fails. Her womb is admirably fertile in itself, but tobacco hinders propagation; and while that is the only Diana of the country, you must expect as little of other commodities as there is worship of God amongst us. Your books, I shall afford you house-room for them and I doubt little else, but there they are to be disposed of at your appointment. Herbert's poems I received and at the opening of it I went into the Church and fell down on my knees to pray for you and your religious family.

" The gloves came also to my hands, but not the silk-worms' eggs. But, sweet gentlewoman, you need not trouble yourself with a way to get us silk. Pride hath done that already, for we will have it, whatsoe'er we pay for it, and did you but see our women that neither card nor spin, how grandly they are attired, you'd almost say that Solomon in all his glory was not clothed like one of these.

"Your father's letter I received not, but pray present my service to him and tell him from me that our sins in Virginia are as ripe for judgment as ever they were in England. And we hear it is coming towards us; for your new Comed-unbuilt State * hath proclaimed us rebels and makes all ships lawful prize that shall trade to us without their licence; and this year, they say, intends to send men of war into our parts. So that, without a speedy turn, Virginia is like to end, as she began, in smoke.

"But God's will be done, though in our undoing; and however it falls, you shall never want one in Virginia who very much honours you, loves your virtues and prays that you may reap the fruits of your everlasting happiness in a better world, while he lives there who takes leave to write himself, Your devoted servant, Edward Johnson.

"From my house in Mulberry Islands Parish upon James River in Virginia." †

This is the only letter from the excellent Mr Johnson; one wishes there were more. An interesting point that does emerge from what he says is that Virginia Ferrar, no doubt under her father's direction, was already showing an active concern in the colony's affairs and had started her experiments in the cultivation of silkworms. She was now a young woman of twenty-two, a vigorous, jolly person, who made friends wherever she went; fond of nice clothes; a dutiful but not notably pious Churchwoman; intelligent and capable, but in no sense bookish—she spelt atrociously to the end of her life; warm-hearted, affectionate, and, like many of her family, gifted with a shrewd business sense.

Such is the fairly clear impression that emerges from the

---

* Presumably a sarcastic play on the word " Commonwealth ".

† Magdalene College MSS; Edward Johnson to Virginia Ferrar, 11 March 1650.

relevant letters and other documents that have survived. She was devoted to her father; and it was during the last ten years of his life, when he was a saddened and weary old man, that she was able to help and relieve him in all sorts of ways, especially in his correspondence with his friends overseas.

As an interesting and curious instance, let us recall the long-prevailing belief, both in this country and in the Atlantic colonies, that the western seaboard of America was only a few days' journey inland from the eastern, and that the opening up of the overland route would provide a direct passage to the East Indies. This belief persisted until quite the later part of the seventeenth century and it was ardently held by John Ferrar. In 1623 the Virginian Assembly in Jamestown recorded its view that a properly equipped expedition should be able to reach the Pacific coast in six days. Nothing, however, was done about it at the time and there appears to have been no further allusion to the project until some twenty-seven years later.

On 20 August 1650 Virginia Ferrar wrote a letter to Lady Berkeley, wife of the newly appointed Governor of the colony. It began with a brief review of the colony's history and with many sanguine opinions about its future. The time has now come, says the letter, to go on " to a most happy discovery for the finding out a short and speedy safe way to the East Indies, part by land and part by rivers and sea to that wealthy place through the continent of Virginia . . . a 10 or 14 days' march westward [at a suit]able time of the year with 50 foot and 30 horse-men, and what is thi[s among] the thousands in Virginia to spare." *

The matter, continues Virginia, is urgent. There is little time to accomplish " this most glorious and wealthy work " which posterity will hail as " the Lady Berkeley's glorious discovery ".

" Madam, I am Virginia. Had I been Virginius, not my poor simple lines should have thus presented themselves unto you, but my person should have attended your noble commands upon this discovery. . . . Give me leave, sweet madam, to tell you

---

* The MS is torn in several places, and I have supplied the probably missing words.

that my name daily calls upon me to pray and wish Virginia prosperity. The love of that place, I may say, is hereditary unto me. My worthy grandfather, one of the first and chief adventurers in this noble Christian design, my much-honoured uncle, my dear father not only much time but the best part of £10,000 hath by our family been expended towards this great and glorious work."

The letter concludes with an urgent plea that colonization should be extended farther southward beyond the River Choanoke " where the sweet sugar, rich indigo, fine cotton, healthful ginger, wealthy silk, pleasant wines, useful rice and cheerful olives and what-not would grow to the infinite and speedy advancing Virginia to the height of all happiness, to a sweet, pleasant, healthy, warm southerly remove rather than to a cold, barren, northerly ".

This eloquent plea, coming from a member of a family so long and honourably associated with the colony, could hardly fail to impress the new Governor and his wife. Perhaps a more sophisticated man than Berkeley might have smiled at its rather naïve enthusiasm. No doubt the pressure of other duties prevented his taking any action when he first reached the colony. But Virginia's letter was not forgotten; for nearly twenty years later, in May 1669, Berkeley wrote home to ask for authority to equip an expedition to proceed inland for the discovery of the East India Sea. He explained that he intended to lead the expedition himself; two thousand gentlemen had volunteered to accompany him, but the plans had been held up by unusually long and heavy rains.

The commission was granted and on 22 May 1670 the party set forth. Berkeley was in poor health and decided that he ought not to go. The expedition had instructions to travel inland till they found streams flowing westward, showing that they had crossed the main watershed. Inevitably their supplies gave out long before they had accomplished their purpose. They were forced to return after an absence of less than three weeks and the attempt was not renewed.

So ends an interesting little byway of American history. The

letter to Lady Berkeley in the Magdalene College collection,
which is, of course, a copy or draft of the one actually sent, is in
John Ferrar's hand with Virginia's signature at the end.   It is
obviously his composition; its style is unmistakably his and is
quite unlike the chatty informality of Virginia's own correspondence.   The same applies to most of the Ferrar letters
which went out to different people in the colony during these last
years of John Ferrar's life; it applies to all the documents dealing
with the cultivation of silkworms.   In all cases it is clear that the
letters were drafted by John in his daughter's name; they were
presumably copied out and signed by her for dispatch to the
person concerned.

The reasons for this procedure may be readily surmised.
John Ferrar enjoyed writing and possessed an unrivalled knowledge of the colony's affairs.   If his style was a little flowery and
occasionally tortuous, he could express himself clearly and
cogently, and it was natural that he should prefer to draft important letters himself, even when he was concerned to describe
experiments which had been conducted by his daughter.   Virginia would have been incapable of writing the kind of reports
that were needed.   But it was she, as it were, who had done all
the work and John wished that she should have all the credit.
The advice given to the colonists should therefore come from
her and in her name.

Moreover, John was astute enough to realize that, in the eyes
of the Virginians, his daughter was a romantic figure.   It would
have been one thing for an elderly man like himself to have urged
Lady Berkeley to explore the overland route to the East Indies;
it was quite another that the challenge should come from a young
girl so fired with enthusiasm that she wished herself a boy only
that she might join in so glorious an enterprise.   There can be
no doubt that Virginia Ferrar was widely and honourably known
in the colony.   Her very name held a high dramatic appeal; the
tone of Edward Johnson's letter, which has just been quoted,
illustrates the affectionate regard in which she was held.   " I
could wish ", he says, " that as Virginia gave you your name, you
could give Virginia your virtues.   'Tis the only plant that is

wanting in that country and I desire you would beg it of God for Virginia in your prayers."

The first efforts to promote the cultivation of silk in Virginia date back to the earliest years of the colony's history.   Those wise and far-sighted men who directed the fortunes of the Virginia Company—Sandys, Danvers, old Mr Ferrar, and, in the Company's last years, such younger men as John and Nicholas Ferrar—had been at pains to secure expert advice and to do everything to encourage the silk industry.   Some initial success had been achieved, but the colony's development had had a disastrous setback in the massacre of 1622 and there is no evidence that the matter was seriously pursued during the years following the liquidation of the Virginia Company.   The colony's development was becoming more and more linked with the cultivation of tobacco, the very thing that the pioneers had striven to prevent.   Nemesis came with the accession of the Commonwealth government at home and the subsequent passing of the first Navigation Act.   These years coincided with a great wave of emigration to the American colonies—between 1649 and 1664 the population of Virginia rose from 15,000 to something over 40,000.   And it was during this period that a sustained effort, of which John Ferrar and Virginia were undoubtedly the moving spirits, was made to re-establish silk-cultivation in the colony on a firm and prosperous basis.

It was a subject to which John had given a great deal of thought over a long period of years.   He had come to the firm conviction that the re-introduction of the silk-growing industry was the key to Virginian prosperity.   With characteristic thoroughness he had set himself to master the technicalities; he had encouraged his daughter to keep silkworms from her early girlhood and had watched with satisfaction her growing skill in handling them.   By the time she was grown up, Virginia had become an expert breeder and experimenter and could place an unrivalled knowledge at the service of friends and other interested persons in the colony.

It would appear that the experiments conducted at Little Gidding over a long period of years led to two fundamental conclusions, which were driven home by Virginia and her father with a wealth of illustration and rhetorical emphasis: first, that the best results were obtained by allowing the silkworms to feed outdoors on mulberry leaves or, in certain cases, on the leaves of other trees; and second, that the native-bred Virginian silkworm was vastly superior in performance to any stock imported from Britain or elsewhere. On the latter point we have amongst the Magdalene papers an interesting broadsheet, of which five hundred printed copies were sent out to the colony in 1654. It is addressed:

" To All the Ingenious Virginia Gentlemen-Planters that are upon the most happy design of a Silk Trade there.

" A Comparison showing the pre-eminence of the rare naturall Virginia silkworm above all others, especially in 2 Particulars. By V.F."

The pamphlet begins by stating the two paramount qualities of the Virginian silkworms: (1) it feeds and thrives on various trees and shrubs besides the mulberry; (2) " whereas a thousand European worms spin but 1 lb. of silk worth at most 30/- a lb., a thousand Virginian worms spin 10 lbs. of silk, rather coarser than the European, but not worth less than 20/- a lb."

" This granted," continues Virginia, " I presume it unnecessary to advise all Virginia planters to make a diligent and narrow search into the adjacent woods for the procurement of as many natural silkworm bottoms [i.e. cocoons] as they can get this winter-time. And carefully to put them up in some box or chest, so that when the fly shall come out in his due time and season, they may couple together, for which care and pains every female fly will lay then of gallant eggs a spoonful whose number must in all probability exceed 500. A wonderful and multiplying creature. And all men may be assured that on what tree soever the bottoms are found, on the leaves of the same tree their offspring will feed and prosper.

" And thus, where there is no want of worms and food (which are the only foundations and materials of silk) there must undeniably follow a most speedy, gallant, easy, infinite, rich trade of silk. Virginia exceedeth the whole world in these particulars of worms and food (neither envy nor malice can gainsay it) besides other great advantages she hath which are needless here to repeat. So that truly that superlative country for that commodity deserves the just title of Empress of all the Silken lands in the world.

" Short is the time of gaining this great wealth, but forty five days, in which space this wonderful creature both feeds and spins her silk, and requires no more of her owners than costless leaves to be given her, which by a strange secret virtue in her nature she converts into silk. And spinning out of her rich belly, with her dainty fine mouth most artificially weaves it into a most curious oval silk-bottom, which again is re-wound by a slight skill of turning only with a man's hand into all pure, perfect silk threads. And for the matter of labour and skill which belong to all this rich design, a child may perform it, as upon trial shall be found most true.

> " No wit nor strength nor purse nor stock shall need,
> But eyes and hands the worms to guard and feed.
> And thus, you see, done is the silken deed
> That brings you so much wealth with so much speed.
> No employment in the world so likely
> To make your lazy savages soon wealthy." *

The hand is the hand of John, who was apt to burst into rhymed couplets in moments of exhilaration, sometimes with even more startlingly banal results than the foregoing. No doubt this spirited little broadsheet served to awake an initial interest in the minds of the planters, but there was evident need for more detailed information, for some short text-book on the whole art of silk cultivation. This was provided in a pamphlet entitled *The Reformed Virginian Silkworm*, which was published anonymously, but which is known to have been the work of that versatile journalist of the period, Samuel Hartlib.† It is on very

---

* " Lazy savages " is almost certainly an allusion to some of the British Colonists and not to the native Indians, of whom the Ferrars always spoke with great sympathy and respect.

† Hartlib first came to England in 1628, and lived in London till his death in 1662; he was probably of Lithuanian parentage. He was a man of original mind who wrote prolifically on many subjects, including bee-keeping, the use of machinery in agriculture, and reforms in education. He also commented on the Apocalypse, looking forward to the fulfilment of all its prophecies in the year 1655, and propounded a scheme for a universal language.

much the same lines as the broadsheet, but considerably fuller. It is quite obviously based on *data* and conclusions supplied by John and Virginia.   Virginia herself is several times mentioned in it.

The Reformed Virginian Silkworm begins by advocating Virginia Ferrar's practice of allowing the silkworms to feed on mulberry leaves in the open air.   It goes on to an eloquent statement of the superiority of the native Virginian silkworm over those of all other countries.   The Virginian worm would feed and flourish on crab-apple, plum, poplar, oak, cherry, and hickory leaves as well as on mulberry.   It was said to produce an outer cocoon ten inches in circumference and six inches long; and within was a second cocoon, in which the worm was wrapped, both cocoons being full of silk.   Virginia had experimented at Gidding with specimens sent from the colony.   She had found that eggs were hatched in nine days, that the worms were fully developed in a month and that in just over six weeks they were capable of spinning silk of such strength that it would hold in a line of several miles long without breaking.   The redoubtable creature was said to produce ten times more silk than the English-bred worm and costs were one-third cheaper.   It was finally mentioned that freight charges were small, since 500 lbs. of silk occupied the same space on shipboard as 10 lbs. of tobacco.

In the meantime a number of successful experiments in silk cultivation were being conducted in the colony itself.   Edward Digges, a wealthy and prominent settler, who corresponded regularly with John and Virginia, told the former in 1654 that he had collected 10 lbs. of eggs, which he intended to distribute to friends who wished to become silk-masters.   He had also, at his own cost, brought out to the colony two Armenian experts for advisory and experimental work.

The arrival of these men in Virginia is celebrated in a long doggerel poem in the Magdalene collection.   It bears the following resounding title :

" Upon the Most Illustrious, Most Noble, Magnificent Natural Virginia Silk Worm : Her wonderful various Plentiful Good, The Infinite Speedy Great Worth she will produce in forty five days with little Labour, Cost and Skill, The Singular Aptness of that Superlative Climate in the breeding them upon so many several trees in her Woods where they live, feed and Spin their Mighty large Strong Bottoms, to the admiration of this our Old World and Glory of Virginia in that New."

Marginally the poem is stated to be " by Ruffe " and is written out in John Ferrar's hand. It traverses the same ground as Hartlib's pamphlet with much rhetorical ornament, and concludes:

> " To the most noble, deserving Squire Digges upon
> the arrival of his two Armenians in Virginia.
> Courage, brave Sir, sith aid from God is sent,
> Proceed, go on, drive forth thy great intent."

Another poem amongst the Magdalene papers is headed " Upon the Silkworm ", and is signed J.B. It is written in a moralizing vein, points a contrast between the industry of the silkworm and the slothful lethargy of man, urges its readers to amendment of life by casting off " that old and rotten Man " as the silkworm casts her skin; and a good deal more in the same homiletic style.

It is clear that behind the stream of correspondence and propaganda about silk-cultivation that came from Little Gidding during these years, there lay a wealth of expert knowledge. John Ferrar had himself invented a method of boiling the hard, sticky cocoons in lye (an alkaline solution of potash) and then immersing them in scalding water, so as to soften their texture and thus ease the process of unwinding the silk. Virginia had kept silkworms since early childhood. Writing to Colonel Yeardley's wife in 1654, she could declare that she spoke " by experience of 20 years' knowledge ". The perseverance and single-minded enthusiasm of father and daughter to encourage this important industry entitle them to an honoured place in the annals of the colony.

And yet the results of all their efforts were extremely disappointing. John must have been aware that he was backing a lost cause; perhaps that knowledge partially accounts for his rhetoric and exaggeration, for the way in which he often so obviously over-called his hand. Certainly his estimate of the possibilities of silk-culture in Virginia was far too sanguine. It is true that the vested interests of the tobacco growers were solidly against him, but there must have been other difficulties as well. Silk culture never gained a real hold in the colony; John Ferrar was its last champion.

Mary Ward (*née* Mapletoft) had, as we have recorded, emigrated to Virginia in 1649. She and Virginia Ferrar kept up a fairly regular correspondence: they had many interests in common and had always been great friends. We learn from Ruffe's doggerel lines that she had taken up the cultivation of silkworms under her cousin's encouragement.

> Lo, hear what Mistress Mary Ward hath sent,
> (Which to her lady cousin she presents)
> Ten rare bottoms took from her apple tree
> That all England may it believe and see.
> Her honoured Kinsman, Esquire Ferrar,
> To conform and make the wonder greater,
> Ten more likewise hath sent her which he found
> On stately oak and shrubs that kiss the ground.

We also have a letter from Mary to Virginia, dating from about this time:

" Sweet cousin," she writes, " I received your kind letter in which you counsel me to set upon the silk trade, which I intend, God permitting me, so to do. You write in your letter that you wonder why I did not wind it myself; the reason was because there was but a small quantity which was not worth the making of a reck for it. I desire you would send me word what is the current price of silk per lb. in bottoms and what is the price if it be wound. My uncle, your father, hath sent me a great many queries about the green fly, which I can say nothing of, but that I had it of an apple tree and brought it and put it in a box and sent it to you; and for the other fly, I had the bottom of an Indian, but this year can get none of neither sort to send you. . . . Please to accept a roll of tobacco from me, it being an emblem of my love." *

This is the last letter in the Magdalene collection from anyone in Virginia to any member of the Little Gidding household.

* Mary Ward to Virginia Ferrar, 14 April 1656.

Mary Ward lost her husband in 1658, and was subsequently married again to a Mr Nathaniel Utye of Maryland. She herself died tragically on 4 October 1665, after being attacked and stabbed by a negro servant.* Whether Virginia Ferrar subsequently continued any of her work with the silkworms it is impossible to say. It is difficult to believe that all her contacts with her colonial friends were allowed to drop after her father's death. Yet it may have been a relief to her to be no longer involved so urgently in colonial matters; even the silkworms must at times have been more of a burden than a pleasure.

* I owe this information to the kindness of the late Mr John D. Collett of Indianapolis. Mr Collet was a direct descendant of the John Collett who emigrated to Virginia in 1650.

VI

A DEEP pathos surrounds the last years of John Ferrar's life. The times, as he wrote to his future son-in-law, were "dangerous, troubled and unsettled", the great causes to which he had given a lifelong devotion seemed irretrievably lost. Casting back in his memory over those years before the coming of the civil war, he could only think of them as a time:

"Of such unheard of and not be to paralleled benefits in all kinds, in the sincerity of religion, the glorious state of our Church, and peace, plenty, and prosperity which universally overflowed the whole kingdom and nation; such a condition we then were in as since the world began no history can produce any nation so long time possessed." *

Often he recalled the prophetic words that Nicholas had spoken shortly before his death, the warnings of sad times coming, of trial and disaster and the destruction of all that they held most precious in the life of the Church and nation. Those words had been most abundantly fulfilled; and yet through every adversity John had remembered his brother's command that they should keep in the "good old way" that he had taught them, the way of devotion and good works which, as Nicholas had declared, was "the right and true way that leadeth to life everlasting". Herein, so far as had lain in his power, John had not failed. The inspiration of his brother's example and leadership had sustained him through the years; and in the evening of his life, in a characteristic memorandum concerning his son's proposed marriage, he could speak of Little Gidding in terms that recall words written twenty years earlier by Lenton and other visitors, "their house and family being the whole parish and they have a minister there . . . one of his nieces † lives in the house . . . on Sundays

* Magdalene College MSS; John Ferrar to his son, n.d.
† i.e., Mary Collett.

87

divine service fully and Communion each first Sunday month, and go daily all the week. . . . Their church stands at the end of their garden near the house." *

Much had had to be given up, but the framework remained, the hallowing of each day by an ordered cycle of worship and the maintenance of many charitable works, as far as John's diminished resources allowed it.   It must have been at about this time that he decided to set down, for his son's guidance, certain instructions and directions for the conduct of affairs at Little Gidding after his own death.   It is the letter of an old man who loves his son, who has known great adversity, bitter disappointment and much personal sorrow, but in whose heart there burns the fire of an unquenchable faith.   It shows in moving terms how searchingly John interpreted the duties of his position as his mother's heir and his brother's successor at Little Gidding; and the passionate conviction with which it is written may reflect an element of doubt that he would never have acknowledged, a lack of absolute assurance that his wishes would be fully respected. Perhaps John may have felt in his heart that with his own death, the real story of Little Gidding would come to a close; so in fact it was to be.

"My most dear and beloved son," he begins, "I hold it my duty to God to declare unto you these things following and take it to be your duty to hearken unto it and to follow my advice in the particulars here expressed, knowing assuredly that what I counsel unto you (and if I may say command you to obey) all is and shall be to your more superlative happiness in this and the other world."

He goes on to recall the monthly thanksgiving that had been instituted at Gidding by " your pious grandmother and devout uncle, the founders of our family and present state " and how he had conceived it a bounden duty to continue that observance and to maintain those charitable works in which they " as is well known to all, during their lives abounded plentifully ".   To this intent he had resolved to set apart each year the twentieth part of his income " as an oblation of praise . . . to some charitable

* Magdalene College MSS; John Ferrar MS; n.d.

and pious uses such as God should present unto me ". This he had carried out as far as circumstances had allowed; its fulfilment during the years of their exile had not been possible, but when Almighty God in His goodness had enabled them to return to their home and inheritance, then he had renewed the resolution and had not been turned from it. He urges upon his son the daily remembrance of God's mercy and the continuance of these pious observances.

" Now, my dear son, let these motives prevail with you with a firm resolution and joyful heart to make a free-will offering to God of the twentieth part of your yearly revenue when God shall see good, after mine and mother's decease, to make you possessor of my estate in Gidding, knowing assuredly that nothing can produce more happiness not only to your soul's good but to your present happiness and worldly prosperity and blessing in this life. Remembering daily those two divine verses of your uncle's most dear friend (of whom it was said by them that knew them both there was one soul in two bodies)—

> Great almsgiving lessens no man's living
> By giving to the poor we increase our store.*

" And I shall leave you a table to be hung up in the house wherein these verses shall be written. Perform what I counsel and be confident of God's and my blessing. Amen, Amen, Amen." †

There was so much to think about, so much to arrange, so many matters to set in order. John's eyes were giving him trouble and he found difficulty in reading or writing by candlelight. But the energy of his mind was still unbounded. There was his Virginian correspondence and the work with the silkworms. Many links with the past remained unbroken and he must have found himself increasingly occupied with his memories of years long gone by. In April 1653 a letter from his old friend Sir John Danvers recalled his mind to those stirring days nearly

---

* The reference is to George Herbert; the lines, not quite accurately quoted, are from Herbert's *Jacula Prudentum*.

† From the MS at Magdalene College. The letter is printed in Blackstone, *The Ferrar Papers*, pp. 300-3.

thirty years earlier, when the Royal Commissioners had ordered the surrender of all the books and records of the Virginia Company and when Nicholas and his nephew Thomas Collett had toiled to make a complete copy of the Court Book, which had been completed with only a week to spare. The two large volumes had been handed to the Earl of Southampton, who had embraced Nicholas delightedly, telling him that " he should esteem them as much more highly than the evidences of his land, as his honour was dearer to him than his estate or his life ".*

Now, thirty years afterwards, Sir John Danvers, a former Virginian adventurer and an old family friend of the Ferrars, writes to John and begins by giving him an invitation to London.

" The often discourse that I have with Capt. Matthews concerning Virginia cannot omit to wish you sometimes in these parts and possibly it wd. refresh you to go home with Capt. Matthews and me on a Friday evening when I bring him back to Westminster on Tuesday morning following.† And now possibly your memory may help me who, enquiring into the present Earl of Southampton's books and papers in the hope of finding the copies of the Lieger Court Books which I had delivered to the former Earl who seemed to store them as his best evidence in that employment, am answered that the late Earl of Devon and Mr. Farrer took all papers and books concerning Virginia and Somers Islands from Southampton House upon the news of the Earl's death in Holland.‡   Now if you can inform or advise me which way these books may be found, I shall hope to make those memorials yet very beneficial towards that Plantation, so much in your thoughts and renewed by the comfort of your good daughter Virginia." §

John Ferrar evidently answered this letter, but he seems to have ignored Sir John's query about the Court Book. Perhaps he did not know the answer; more probably, I think, he had

* Mayor, op. cit., p. 216.
† One of the earliest examples, surely, of a week-end invitation !
‡ In 1624.
§ Magdalene College MSS; Sir John Danvers to John Ferrar, 8 April 1653.

information which he did not wish to reveal. A month later Danvers writes again:

"My satisfaction had been more particular and better if I would know where to find those books and papers that were taken from Southampton House in Holborn immediately after the news of that noble Earl's death, which his lordship's steward affirms were taken thence by the then Earl of Devonshire and Mr. Farrer, which I supposed could not be other than your brother or self. But if therein you remember nothing, your further trouble on that occasion is spared." *

If John Ferrar did know what had happened to the Court Book and other Virginian papers, he was to die without revealing it. Peckard, writing nearly one hundred and forty years later, says that the first Earl of Southampton was advised not to keep the volumes in his own house, and accordingly gave them into the custody of Sir Robert Killegrew, who kept them till he died and left them to the Earl of Dorset. "It is hoped", adds Peckard, "that this noble family still hath them in safe keeping." †

This is presumably based on information contained in the Ferrar family papers which Peckard inherited when he married Martha Ferrar, and we have no reason to doubt its truth. But it is certain that the Court Book copy was no longer in the possession of the Earl of Dorset's family in Peckard's time. The Earl of whom Peckard speaks died in 1652; twenty years later, in 1673, the two volumes of the Court Book were purchased from the Earl of Southampton's estate by Colonel William Byrd for sixty guineas, so that they had clearly been restored in the meantime, perhaps under the Earl of Dorset's will, to the Southampton family. As is well known, the volumes are now in the Library of Congress.

It was at about this time that John came to hear of another matter which roused his keenest interest. Early in 1653 plans were announced and subscriptions invited for the publication of a Polyglot Bible under the editorship of Dr Brian Walton. A

---

* Magdalene College MSS; Sir John Danvers to John Ferrar, 7 May 1653.
† Peckard, op. cit., p. 156.

number of distinguished theologians and scholars had promised their collaboration; they included Archbishop Ussher, Dr Thorndike, Dr Lightfoot, Abraham Wheelock, the first professor of Arabic at Cambridge, Dr Robert Sanderson and others. The complete work was to be published in five volumes; the first would contain the Pentateuch in the Hebrew, Septuagint Greek, and Vulgate Latin texts; Volumes II and III would cover the rest of the Old Testament in the same three languages; Volume IV would contain the Apocrypha in Greek, Latin, Syriac, and Arabic, with an additional Hebrew text of the Book of Tobit; in Volume V would be given the New Testament in Latin, Greek, Syriac, Arabic, and Ethiopic, together with a Persic text of the Gospels; Volume VI would consist of chronological tables, critical notes, geographical charts, tables of weights and measures, and other explanatory matter.

The project seems to have been warmly welcomed. By May 1653 more than £9,000 had been promised in subscriptions. Printing was started in October of that year and the first volume appeared in 1654, the others following at approximately annual intervals thereafter. Such was the inception of what Dr Walton's biographer described as: " a work vastly exceeding all former attempts of that kind and that came so near perfection as to discourage all future ones ".*

It was natural that John Ferrar should be much interested in the project from the start. He had good reason to think that he might be able to offer the compilers some valuable help; for he had in his possession a number of Biblical texts in foreign languages which had been used by his younger son Nicholas, together with all the papers and notes that that brilliant young scholar had left behind him. In particular, he still had at Gidding the New Testament in twenty-four languages which had been shown, but never presented, to King Charles I. Corresponding with his old friend Richard Drake, who was one of Dr Walton's assistants, he eagerly offered the use of any texts that might be of help to the compilers. He suggested the addition of

* H. J. Todd, *Memoirs of the Life and Writings of the Rt. Rev. Brian Walton, D.D.*, etc. (London, 1821), Vol. I, p. 72.

an Armenian version of some of the sacred books; he would evidently have liked to see a number of other languages included. Drake was duly appreciative:

" Worthy Sir," he writes, " The great affection you have showed for the promoting of the edition of the Bible in divers languages is a singular argument of your ingenuous and public spirit."

He goes on, however, to explain that the editors' design is to preserve only the most ancient and authoritative texts, and that it would be difficult for that reason to make use of later translations, such as those which his friend had to offer.

" Yet because you are so ready to afford your assistance in the advance thereof, it is desired that if you have any ancient Saxon or Gothic translations of any part of the text, you would be pleased to communicate them; for there may be use haply made of them, though not in the body, yet in the appendix of the work. We say as much of your work on the New Testament in 24 languages; the comparing of them with other copies may afford some light and beauty to the work." *

It is interesting to know that the younger Nicholas's amazing multilingual version of the New Testament may have been used, if only for purposes of comparison and for the adding of " light and beauty " to their work, by the compilers of the London Polyglot. No other correspondence survives to throw further light on the matter. There is only a short letter from Drake, nearly two years later, reminding John that the fourth instalment of his subscription has fallen due and that, on payment of it " the third tome will be delivered to you by Dr. Walton at the Printing House in Charterhouse Yard ".†

John may have been disappointed that more use was not made of his son's translations, though he would have readily appreciated the reasons. During these last years of his life he was living more and more upon the memories of bygone days. Seen in retrospect, the past was so rich and full of blessing; the present, to quote Shirley's epitaph, was a time when " all things sacred

---

* Magdalene College MSS; Richard Drake to John Ferrar, 26 May 1653.
† Ibid., 19 March 1655.

throughout the land were either demollisht or profaned "; of
the future he only thought in terms of the things unseen and
eternal. In 1652 Herbert's *Country Parson* was published with
an introduction by Barnabas Oley, who spoke in affectionate and
moving terms of Nicholas Ferrar, of the loving friendship that
had united him with Herbert, and of his holy and devoted life at
Little Gidding. Perhaps it was this short memoir that determined John to set about a task that no one but himself could
undertake satisfactorily; from the wealth and intimacy of his
own memories he would write what he knew of his brother's
life. He would tell the whole story. He would describe how
the family had first come to Little Gidding and how their way of
life had been worked out under Nicholas's direction into a golden
sequence of worship and service. A vast collection of family
papers were at hand to refresh his memory and to colour the
details of his narrative. Nicholas, quite simply, was the best and
wisest man he had ever known; he had always felt for him a
devotion bordering on veneration. Was it not a clear duty, in
his own latter days, to pay what tribute he could to his revered
brother's memory?

John's short life of Nicholas is the primary source of our knowledge of the Little Gidding community. It was probably written
during the years 1653 and 1654, and the manuscript remained with
the family papers at Gidding for many years after John's death.
Towards the end of the seventeenth century large portions of it
were transcribed by Thomas Baker, the Cambridge antiquary.
The manuscript itself, along with the whole collection of Ferrar
documents, came into the possession of Dr Peter Peckard, Master
of Magdalene College, Cambridge, by his marriage to John
Ferrar's great-grand-daughter, Martha. Those familiar with the
Little Gidding story will remember that Peckard lent this and
other manuscripts to a Hertfordshire clergyman, the Reverend
John Jones, who never returned them. They have not been
traced and it seems unlikely that they will ever be found again.

Two surviving manuscripts—the Almack MS in the Cambridge
University Library (Add. MSS 4484) and the Jones MS at Dr
Williams's Library, London (Jones MS B. 87)—contain passages

almost certainly transcribed from the original. Baker's transcript (Cambridge University Library, Baker MSS, Vol. 35) probably gives us all the most important matter; at any rate, the sections dealing with Little Gidding seem to be substantially complete. But we cannot be certain; the fact remains that John Ferrar's original script must be regarded as irretrievably lost. But it was not until nearly two hundred years after its composition that a printed version appeared. This was in the volume *Two Lives of Nicholas Ferrar*, published in 1855 under Professor Mayor's editorship; it contained the text of the Baker transcript and of the later life of Nicholas by Bishop Turner of Ely, adapted by Dr Jebb. In recent years Dr Blackstone, making use with great critical skill of all the available MS material, has given us, as nearly as is now possible, the full text of the original life.* It is, however, readily apparent that there are gaps in the narrative which cannot be filled.

The text as we now have it runs to some 50,000 words. It is written in a casual and episodic manner; had John revised it after his first draft, he must, one feels, have done a good deal of re-arrangement and disposed his material in more orderly fashion. It is an old man who is jotting down his reminiscences, recalling many episodes and impressions that are vividly stamped in his memory; but the sequence of events is often lost, for one recollection suggests an earlier one and you get paragraphs beginning with such phrases as "I forgot to say" and similar inconsequences. There is no attempt at literary grace in John's style of writing. His long sentences, sometimes extending over half a page or more, are apt to lose themselves in a jungle of subordinate clauses from which the author can extricate himself only by an exhausted parenthesis, as a man might pause to take breath before resuming his train of thought. Yet the book does not make difficult reading; for the most part, John writes simply and vividly, without artifice, his narrative carried along by his passionate earnestness to set down the wonderful story that he has to tell. Many seventeenth-century Englishmen wrote English prose as well as it has ever been written. Even those,

* B. Blackstone, *The Ferrar Papers* (Cambridge, 1938).

like John, who made no pretence to literary gifts, were unable to write badly. Always their language had a certain aptness and limpidity which made it readable and lively.

John Ferrar was a man of his time in his unfailing serious-ness of mind; there was, perhaps, a strong puritanical element in his nature. He has none of that lightness of touch that we find so delightfully in Izaak Walton's *Lives* or in Fuller. His occasional touches of humour are entirely unintentional, as when, in speaking of his mother's fondness for good preaching, he relates that she had in her lifetime heard 12,000 sermons, " for she was also addicted that way ". Where Little Gidding is concerned, he is inclined to see things through lenses of high magnification. Visitors to Gidding numbered " not hundreds, but some thousands . . . many were of the best in the land both of men and women, persons of great quality ". When Bishop Williams comes to hold a Confirmation, one has the impression of a vast concourse assembling from all the neighbouring towns for the occasion. The meetings of the family study-circle which they called the " Little Academy " are described in terms that suggest the deliberations of some important learned society. Memory invests the past with this aura of grandeur and John was only recording his own sincere impressions.

One of the qualities that makes John's work so moving is his own complete selflessness. No biographer was ever more humble or self-effacing. John always refers to himself in the third person. The book is about Nicholas, and John is " his brother " or sometimes " J.F."; the personal pronoun occurs nowhere from beginning to end. Nicholas had been his hero and pattern; always it had been his greatest happiness to act as Nicholas wished; separation from him had been unendurable; Nicholas's strength and wisdom and flaming purity of heart had been the sustaining power of his own life. Those twelve golden years from the family's first coming to Gidding until Nicholas's death had indeed been years of blessing; there had been trials and difficulties of many kinds, but how could they be counted against all the joys of family life, all the graces that had been poured upon them in their willing service of God? John's description of life and worship at Little Gidding, in its utterly simple sincerity, marvellously conveys that sense of serenity and peace and happiness which impressed those visitors and friends who came, for long or short periods, to share in it. The witness of men like Oley and Walton and Robert Mapletoft and Edmund Duncon is sufficient to show that John Ferrar wrote no less than the truth and that the Little Gidding household was indeed a " congregation of saints ".

It was not until the papers at Magdalene College came to light in 1935 that we knew anything of those troubles and discords and frictions from which no society of human beings can be free. From motives of loyalty and charity John Ferrar resolved to say nothing whatever about such things. We hear nothing from him of the anxieties caused by some of the younger members of the family, of the constant sponging and importunity of Richard Ferrar, of Margaret Collett's wilfulness, of the difficult and tiresome children who were received from time to time at Gidding and who defied all attempts to train them in better ways. In John's narrative there is no breath of discord from beginning to end. It is, I think, a sign of his marvellous forbearance that he says nothing at all of those appalling conflicts that must have tormented his own life and at times worn him almost to breaking-point. For we now know how bitterly his wife resented what she regarded as his subservience to Nicholas and how utterly unable she was to share in the vocation of the family. Bathsheba Ferrar is a pathetic figure; she was not a religiously minded woman and she must always have found life at Little Gidding intolerably irksome. Occasionally her frustration and her distaste of a way of life that she hated, flared out in frenzied outbursts of temper; always she must have been moody and discontented. She was fond of her husband and children, but at Little Gidding she could find no happiness. Even the gentleness and forbearance with which John always treated her may have aggravated her sense of grievance; she must often have felt that she was being treated with the kindly firmness reserved for naughty children, when a flaming row would have been a greater relief to frayed nerves and tempers.

Of all this John gives no hint. His memoir is quite simply a panegyric of Nicholas. He gives us a detailed and satisfying portrait which arrests us by its manifest fidelity. " Enthusiastic admiration ", said Blake, " is the first principle of knowledge and the last." Anyone of the meanest vision can display another man's faults and imperfections. Our failings and vices belong to our human heritage and, with differences of degree and emphasis, we all share them and most readily recognize them in others. But great virtue is rare and can pass unrecognized. It is to John Ferrar that we owe our knowledge of his brother, not only as a man of high talent and amazingly versatile gifts, but as a servant of God and a burning and shining light in the annals of the Church of England. It is through John's simple and always vivid descriptions of the daily life and occupations of the Little Gidding household that we know more about this family than about any other English family of the period. All subsequent biographies derive from his; all the ancillary material, the *Story Books*, the short memoirs of Oley and Walton, the family letters, the surviving Concordances, serve only to enrich and fill in the details of a picture already drawn. As we read his pages, as we read, in particular, such passages as those describing Nicholas's ordination at Westminster or the truly magnificent and inspired account of his last illness and his holy death, we realize something of the writer's own greatness and nobility of soul.

Perhaps John Ferrar's outstanding quality was the great virtue of fortitude. He possessed none of those commanding talents that had distinguished his younger brother; he was essentially a disciple, not a leader. In some ways, perhaps, he may have been narrow-minded; he may not always have been easy to live with, for he could be fussy and uncompromising. He was inclined to judge by the letter; he liked to have everything put down in writing, and this habit was due as much to a certain inflexibility of mind as to a desire for precision. But if ever a man had fought the good fight and most earnestly sought to lay hold on eternal life, it was John Ferrar. He was a great Churchman, a devoted Christian, a man whose faith and loyalty were never dimmed by the most terrible trials. Sensitive and affectionate by nature, he was kindly and conciliatory in all his intentions. The ideals to which he gave his life and which he followed with such magnificent stedfastness, were the highest ever set before humanity; they were nothing less than the ideals of Christian perfection which have found, all through the centuries, such rich and varied expression and which had inspired the whole achievement of Little Gidding.

In the spring of 1657 John Ferrar's son became engaged to Ann Brook, a young lady whose family lived in Lincolnshire. She came to stay at Gidding and John was delighted with her.

" Such is her lovely, discreet, vertuous, pious deportment ", he wrote to one of her relatives, " that she ravishes my heart with much love and gains the affection and good wishes of all friends and strangers also that see, know and hear of her actions. Happy and thrice happy is my dear son in her consortship and myself blessed in my old age to see and behold and possess this noble Brook from whence (my daily prayers are) there may issue and flow many lovely, pleasant, sweet, virtuous springs that may by their piety and worth change the name of now Little to be Great Gidding in due time." *

The wedding took place at the bride's home and John wrote shortly afterwards to the bride, expressing the earnest hope that she and her husband would come and make their home at Gidding. He assured her of the warmest welcome and especially emphasized the joy that her coming would bring him, because he had understood that there had been doubts in her mind and she had expressed unwillingness to accede to his wish. It is clear enough that some disagreements had already arisen and we can easily enough understand the unreadiness of the young bride to join her " in-laws " in a household where things followed a very definite pattern. Her reply to her father-in-law was courteous and dutiful, but uncompromising; she and her husband were quite resolved to remain in the house they had taken at Aldekirk. The last of John Ferrar's letters that have survived is a pathetic further appeal to Ann to reconsider her decision, deploring the

---

* Magdalene College MSS; John Ferrar to Mrs Goodwith Beridge, May 1657.

misunderstandings that have arisen. It is undated, but cannot have been written more than three weeks before his death.

We do not know the circumstances in which he died. There can have been no long illness. Death came to him on 28 September 1657, and, as had been directed by Nicholas, he was buried in the space left for his grave between Nicholas's tomb and the west door of the church. Within a month two further bereavements came to the family; John's and Nicholas's sister, Mrs Collett, died on 9 October, and her daughter Susanna Chedley passed away on 31 October. Both are buried at Little Gidding. It was more than the ending of a chapter; it was the end of the story of Little Gidding.

There is a pathetic little epilogue in a letter written on 3 November by John Ferrar *junior* to his wife. He had left home for London and had stopped at Gidding on his way. It was on a Friday; he found his mother in evident distress of mind and declaring her firm and absolute resolve to leave Gidding on Monday, " for an hour longer she would not stay ".

" Upon this information ", he goes on, " I was forced to alter my former intentions of going so soon for London and use my utmost endeavours to take care for a speedy passage for her." Accordingly, he had, on the Saturday, gone over to Oundle to secure a place for her in the coach, only to find that no coach was running that week. He then went to Huntingdon, where he learnt that a wagon would be going up on Monday, but no coach; he travelled on to Peterborough and was told that all seats on the coach from that city were taken. He eventually got home between ten and eleven o'clock at night.

" Next morning I went to her to let her know what I had done, and that unless she would be pleased to stay another week, she could not go up in a coach, but in a wagon. That is best of all, saith she, I had rather go in a wagon than a coach, and go I will by God's help. So upon Monday I carried her to Huntingdon and hired a place for her and myself, and so after a tedious journey and well shaking of my bones we came safe to London upon Wednesday. My mother was very weak and ill in coming up that I much doubted she would never see London; but I bless

God the very sight hath cheered her up and she is at present reasonably well." *

Bathsheba was to live for two years more and we can believe that, after the bitterness of what she must always have felt as the intolerable exile of Little Gidding, her last days were peaceful and contented. She had never ceased to be a Londoner at heart.

* Magdalene College MSS; John Ferrar to his wife, 3 November 1657.

VII

OF the original company that had come to Little Gidding more than thirty years previously, only Mary Collet remained. It was very soon apparent that her small income was inadequate to maintain her there. In August 1658 she was corresponding with her lawyer cousin, Basil Beridge, about the sale of her estate; and it was probably quite soon after this that she left Gidding for good and went to live in her brother Thomas's house in Highgate. Here she was to spend the remaining years of her life.

Virginia Ferrar was now a woman of thirty. She had a small house of her own on the Little Gidding estate and under her father's will she seems to have inherited property in the Bermuda Islands. The rent came to her from a resident tenant; but soon after her father's death she decided that the estate was a poor investment and had best be disposed of. The suggestion made to her by her cousin Nicholas Collett, who acted as her business adviser during these years, was that the tenant should be given the first option of purchasing the land, if he so wished.

"If you intend a letter to your tenant," writes Collett, "you must send it this week, for the ships are ready to go. I conceive you had best sell your land, considering the trouble and little advantage you have of it. If you therefore know of your tenant what he will give you for it and what assurances for your money, you will let him have it before another because he desires it. Truly I believe £20 will be the most you will have for it."

Virginia thought she ought to do better and told her tenant he could have the property for £25. Later Collett writes again:

"Good cousin, By the enclosed from your Bermudas tenant you will understand that he hath accepted your offer for the sale of your land at the price you willed me to propose unto him. Yet withal I perceive he would gladly have somewhat abated him

of £25, if your charity will move you thereto.   I conceived him
a fitting object thereof, for I am informed that he is a very honest
though poor man."

Continuing, he says that he is sending down to Gidding various
things that he had evidently been asked to buy in London.

" But for the chest of oranges he mentioneth, I thought it not
fit to take them up, for they would not have half defrayed the
charges, they all proving so bad this year by reason of the tedious
passage they have had." *

A third letter from Nicholas reports the concluding stages of
the negotiations.

" Worthy cousin, By yours received this week I perfectly
understand your mind and expectations that no less than £25
will satisfy you for your Bermudas land.   I shall not therefore
any farther press you to abatement;   only, as I wrote you the last
week, I feared we should not raise the whole sum presently.   Yet
I find upon farther progress in the matter that we shall now come
somewhat near, for tobacco this year proving better than ordinarily
and come to a pretty good market, so that I have adventured to
take the tobacco he sent upon myself, which weighs near a
thousand weight which I have sold (though not yet fully made up
the a/c) at 6d per lb. which would have made the sum, were it not
for waste and tret with other such dues to be allowed, which I
hope will not be above 30 or 40s;† so that I hope about £23,
which is a small matter more or less, I shall have ready for you
by the time I shall have gotten the consignment made, which
both you and your brother must seal too.   Besides, there will be
50 odd shillings coming to you upon your own rent." ‡

Collett, himself a shrewd enough man of business, evidently
felt that Virginia should have been a little more generous in this
particular deal.   In fact, when it came to the final settlement
and when all but £2 of the purchase money had been received

* He also speaks of " some small parcels directed to Sister Mary Collett;
you will please give them unto her ".   This shows that Mary was still at
Gidding and enables us to date the letter approximately.

† Tret—an allowance to purchasers of 4 lb. for wastage on every
104 lb.

‡ These letters are at Magdalene College.

from the tenant, he told Virginia that, rather than continue pressing "the poor man" for this remaining sum, he would pay it himself.

Whatever light this incident may shed on Virginia's character, it certainly displays the integrity, as well as the kindliness of heart, of Nicholas Collett.   During these years the family owed a great deal to his tact, his wisdom and his truly Christian skill in composing more than one family quarrel.   He was now a middle-aged man; and it may be remembered how, having come to Gidding with his parents in the early days and passed some five years of his boyhood there, he had been apprenticed to Arthur Woodnoth, in whose house he had lived in London until his marriage.   Woodnoth had come to look upon him almost as his own son.   He was loved and trusted by every member of the family; and when Woodnoth died, he became to the Little Gidding household exactly what Woodnoth had been for so many years.   He acted as their business and legal representative as need arose.   He was asked for advice on all sorts of private and domestic matters.   All the family correspondence with America probably passed through his hands.   He was constantly executing orders for them in London, buying provisions, household articles, clothes and so forth, just as Arthur had done. Now he is sending down a small crate of oranges and lemons as a present; he arranges for the satisfactory apprenticing of John Ferrar's grandson in London; he regretfully declines an invitation to Little Gidding because of shortage of staff in his office, "my ushers being yet too green to manage my affairs"; he sends John Ferrar *junior* a new seal with his coat of arms cut in silver.

Some time shortly after John Ferrar's death, a violent quarrel broke out between his son John and a cousin, Benjamin Woodnoth.   It was a sordid enough affair, a dispute about money owed by Benjamin to John—all very unedifying and unpleasant. John Ferrar *junior*, who had succeeded his father as lord of the manor, was in no sense whatever an inheritor of the spirit of Little Gidding; he was just a decent, ordinary man who let his estates down badly by neglect and improvidence, who respected Christian conventions, retained the affection of his wife and children through a very long lifetime, squabbled and grumbled and asserted himself against others like any normal member of the human race, and eventually died in his ninetieth year, having been churchwarden of Little Gidding for more than half a century.   Fortunately for him, he was fond of his cousin and respected his advice; and the quarrel with Woodnoth does illustrate the tact and firmness with which Nicholas Collett handled his affairs.   Nicholas strove by every means to effect a reconciliation, rebuking John for his hard and unreasonable attitude in the matter and telling both parties that, in the heat of personal animosity, they were guilty of magnifying the real differences between them.

"I do therefore heartily wish that you would cast aside this jealousy of each other," he writes to John, "and treat upon friendy terms, that you would make up the a/c of what is due unto him and send him this £28 12s. . . . But till then you will have no further answer of him but a suit which, when begun, I fear will be repented, that you will then come off with much more loss besides the discomposure of your mind, and breach, I fear, of charity to each other, which will be a great offence against the divine Majesty." *

We do not know how the matter ended; it is anyhow of little importance.   But there is real interest in this brief glimpse of Nicholas Collett; in the years after the death of their father, Virginia Ferrar and her brother must have owed a great deal to this wise, peaceable, and kindly man.   The fact that he was some fifteen years their senior enabled him, when occasion called for it, to speak with an avuncular freedom that was always for their good.   Here, for instance, is another of his letters to John, written when the latter had evidently landed himself in some trouble through extravagance or other stupidity.

"We much lament your great trouble wherein you are fallen and condole with you in your bad fortune, which your too great indulgence hath in some measure brought upon you.   But I hope your wisdom will with patience undergo what God hath suffered to come upon you; and seeing what is past cannot be recalled,

* Nicholas Collett to John Ferrar *junior*, n.d.

H

you will look before and providently prevent, as much as you may, future evil. I beseech you, suffer not your passion to get too much hold upon you. Alas, Sir, these crosses are natural to the sons of men and chiefly to the sons of God, and do you expect exemption from the common fate of all? If in this life were all our hope, we were of all men most miserable."

We may refer briefly to certain fragments of correspondence which tell us a little more of Virginia Ferrar's life and activities. She was not often able to visit London, and in the choice of clothes and dress materials she had to rely on the good offices of Anna Mapletoft and her aunt, Margaret Legatt. To the latter she writes:

"I received your kind letter for which I give you humble thanks and for your intimation giving me notice that there is such a gown to be sold which you think will fit me well. I take it for a great favour. I shall entreat you to be pleased to send me soon the next week the hair colour sasnet (*sic*) petticoat and waistcoat you mentioned in your letter, if it be fashionable and like to fit me. . . . I doubt the silver lace may not be so fashionable, though it be very rich, and then it will not be of so good an esteem. I shall therefore only desire the hair coloured petticoat and waist-coat at present."

On another occasion Anna Mapletoft is asked to send down "a stuff morning coat of about 13 or 14 shillings price; half an ell of light green sarcenet of about half an ell wide; 5 yards of ban-galle; a grey goss hood; a black allomode hood; a quarter of a lb. of head powder; a pair of strong buttons for sleeves; half a dozen orings ".*

These letters probably date from the 1660's, and the memories of the earlier years were still fresh and fragrant in the minds of those who shared them. John and Anna Mapletoft had been brought up at Gidding by Mary Collett and could look back to the days when their uncle Nicholas was still living. Others like

* Sarsanet was a silken material, used chiefly for the linings of coats, etc. "Ban-galle" is presumably the striped gingham which was imported from Bengal; "alamode" was the name of a light, glossy black silk.
"Orings" are presumably oranges.

the Kestian and Legatt children, the families of Hester and Margaret Collett respectively, had been accustomed to visit Gidding regularly and to stay occasionally for long periods. To all of them Little Gidding remained something of a wonderland, a place of golden memories, a haven of happiness and tranquillity.

" I never lived a happier life than I lived at Gidding ", writes Anna to her cousin Virginia in a letter of 14 February 1663. And Elizabeth Kestian, nearly twenty years later, confesses that " I love no place in the world like Gidding ", adding that her Aunt Margaret Legatt constantly longs to be able to return there. Virginia herself, happy in the possession of her own small house on the Little Gidding estate, never ceased to cherish the memories of those earlier days. There is one of the rare glimpses of her deeper feelings in a letter written to Mary Collett, after a visit to her Highgate home. She thanks her aunt for having allowed her to come and stay, gives her some news of affairs at Gidding and concludes:

" Let me desire a favour of you, that you would please to give me my dear father's picture to have in my chamber. The remembrance of him is as dear to me as my life, and the sight of him most precious. Therefore I am very ambitious of it."

Virginia seems to have kept in regular touch with her London relatives and she enjoyed an occasional visit to the metropolis. No doubt she stayed more than once at Highgate and also saw a certain amount of the Kestian–Legatt branches of the family, who lived in Westminster and later at Clapham. Elizabeth Kestian and Mary Legatt had started a private school in Lambeth and had taken a house in Westminster, " very airy with a long garden ", to make a home for Mary's mother. The school flourished and it may have been the need of larger premises that prompted them to move into the country suburb of Clapham.

" My cousin Kestian and her family ", writes Richard Ferrar, " are removed from Lambeth to a place called Clapham, about 2 miles from Lambeth, to a much larger house, with hopes of a great addition of scholars." *

It must have been soon after the migration that Virginia went

* Richard Ferrar to his cousin, John Ferrar, 16 January 1673.

to stay with them at Clapham.   We have a letter written by her to her sister-in-law at Gidding.

" You may perhaps wonder that you have not had your things before this time.   Truly the fault was not mine but the tailor's, for they pretend they cannot get men to work with them, so many are gone to sea and others afraid of being pressed that they dare not come to London, for here is great pressing every week to go to sea."

However, the clothes are at last ready, and she is sending them. She hopes they are not too expensive, " I never paid so dear in all my life for making up a plain gown for myself as I have done this time ".

As to the school, Betty Kestian has told her that, " They have £20 a year for every scholar they learn, and they may learn all things, namely, to sing, play, dance, write, learn French, all for £20."

It was evidently a boarding school of a rather exclusive kind, for these are pretty high fees; £20 per annum would correspond to at least £250 in modern currency.   On this occasion Virginia had a specific purpose in visiting the school; for she had, in the goodness of her heart, made herself responsible for the education of one of her nieces and she was now bringing the child down for her first term.

Probably this was in 1673 or 1674, the allusion to press-gang activities suggesting that the third Dutch War was still in progress.   Never were English ships manned by such heterogeneous and ill-trained crews as during these campaigns.   Some of the conscripts were no more than children.   They came from every circumstance and walk of life.   After the great naval engagement of June 1666 it had been observed that many English sailors swimming in the water were still wearing the black Sunday suits in which the press-gang had seized them as they were coming out of church.

Virginia was at Clapham again for a fairly long visit in the summer of 1677.   She tells Anne Ferrar that Mary Collett had been seriously ill and that Dr John Mapletoft had had to travel down to Ely to see his uncle, the Dean, who " lieth very weak ".* Robert Mapletoft was in fact in his last illness; he died only a few days later.

Virginia had been shopping and she reports unfavourably on some silk crape that her sister-in-law had enquired about. She asks Anne to send her up 9 or 10 lb. of butter, and her brother is asked to send £20.

" I pray put it up in the wooden kit (I think you have it) and save the money in a clean lining cloth and put it into the butter and tie the kit up with a small cord and seal it upon the cord; I hope it will come safe to me." †

One hopes it did, with the £20 duly enshrined in the butter. This is the last of Virginia's dated letters. Probably she visited her Clapham cousins each summer; her allusions in another letter to Anne suggest that she was with them in August or September 1678 when popular hysteria over the Popish Plot was at its height.

" I know you hear in the country what discoveries are made every day of the papists and their plots against the King and Kingdom. The Tower is full of noblemen and other sharers in the plot. The city is full of soldiers and all the train band stand upon the guard every day and night. The parliament set very close day and most part of the night. I pray God grant they may find out all those wicked conspirators against the Kingdom."

And here our narrative, as revealed in this great collection of family letters, begins to draw to its close. Mary Collett, now in her eightieth year, died in November 1680, and her funeral took place at Little Gidding. So passed to her rest a great and saintly figure in the annals of the Church of England. It is sad to record that John Ferrar *junior* tried to dispute her will to his own advantage, and had to be firmly put right by Nicholas Collett, acting as her executor.‡

Virginia lived on at Gidding for some years more. She died in January 1687–8 and was buried in the churchyard, in soil already hallowed by the bodies of those whom she had known

---

* Magdalene College MSS; Virginia Ferrar to Anne Ferrar, 16 August 1677.

† Ibid.   ‡ Nicholas Collett to John Ferrar, 2 December 1680.

most intimately and loved most devotedly in her lifetime.   One
could find for her no pleasanter epitaph than the words of one of
her cousins, who is quoted as saying that " she would be heartily
glad to see you, for she says you are the best company that ever
she see, my dear ".

At the manor-house John Ferrar *junior's* long life continued
uneventfully.   He was a kindly man in his own household, but
improvident in practical affairs and inclined to be quarrelsome.
His life was that of the ordinary country gentleman of the period.
Little Gidding was still a parish church and Sunday services were
maintained.   But there is no suggestion that the " good old
way " of family worship was continued.   That was a thing of the
past and no member of the family had any desire for its restoration.   Yet the spirit of Little Gidding was still a living thing;
its continuing inspiration was to be strikingly shown in the long
life of that great English Churchman, Dr John Mapletoft.   He
was John Ferrar *junior's* almost exact contemporary;   they were
born and died within a few months of one another, the one dying
in his ninetieth and the other in his ninety-first year.

John Mapletoft was born on 15 June 1631 at Margaretting in
Essex, of which parish his father, the Reverend Joshua Mapletoft,
was vicar.   His mother Susanna, *née* Collett, was Nicholas
Ferrar's niece.   When his father died in 1635, he was received
into the family at Little Gidding and brought up there under the
direction of his uncle Nicholas, who was also his godfather.
When, after the outbreak of civil war, John Ferrar was compelled
to go abroad, John Mapletoft went to Westminister School, then
under the headmastership of the great Dr Busby.   He came up
to Trinity College, Cambridge, in 1648, took his bachelor's
degree three years later and in 1653 was elected to a fellowship.
The early years of his career show a curious correspondence
with that of his uncle Nicholas of blessed memory.   He resided
for some five years and then went as tutor to the Earl of Northumberland's son.   In 1660 he went abroad to qualify himself as
a physician.   For a year he studied in Rome, where he lived
with the Hon. Algernon Sidney;   he may have continued his
studies at Padua and elsewhere, and returned to England in 1663.

Four years later he took his medical doctorate at Cambridge and settled down to practise as a physician in London.

There can be no doubt that he was a man of high ability and that he soon became a distinguished member of his profession. In July 1669 he was incorporated doctor of physic at Oxford. In the autumn of that year he was invited to accompany the Earl of Essex to Denmark and it was shortly before his departure on this mission that he wrote to John Ferrar with some advice about a prescription against the scurvy.

" I presume you have heard ", he says, " that I am going into Denmark with the King's ambassador thither, my Lord of Essex and cannot hope to be here again before the next spring. . . . My due respects to my good cousin your wife and my cousin Virginia and all your little fry." *

He must have been a man of very winning personality. In London he was on terms of close friendship with Halley, the astronomer, and with such Churchmen as Tillotson, Sherlock, and Stillingfleet; he corresponded intimately with John Locke. He was held in high regard by Sydenham, perhaps the outstanding medical man of his time, who prefaced his great standard work— the Latin treatise, *Medical Observations on the history and treatment of acute diseases*—with a long and affectionate dedication to Mapletoft. A further distinction, which withdrew him from ordinary medical practice, came to him in 1675, when he was appointed professor of physic at Gresham College, the chair that had been held in earlier years by Nicholas Ferrar's friend, Thomas Winston. A few months later he was elected a Fellow of the Royal Society.

He remained at Gresham College for four years. He was now in early middle age, with an assured reputation and with years of useful and congenial work to look forward to in a post of of high distinction. But things were to turn out very differently. In the autumn of 1679 he resigned his professorship and, a fortnight later, married a Miss Rebecca Knightley. We do not know how long or in what circumstances his mind had been

* Magdalene College MSS; John Mapletoft to John Ferrar, 7 September 1669.

drawn to the courses he was now to follow. From the time of his marriage he gave up the practice of medicine altogether and set himself to the serious study of divinity. In March 1682 he was ordained deacon and priest on the same day, and was soon after presented to a small country living in Northamptonshire. Two years later, without any initiative on his part, he was invited to become vicar of St Lawrence Jewry in the City of London; and here he remained, refusing all offers of preferment, for nearly thirty years until his retirement in 1711, when he was more than eighty years of age. His last years were spent in the home of his daughter Elizabeth, wife of Dr Gastrell, Bishop of Chester; he died in Westminster on 10 November 1721 in his ninety-first year.

He received the doctorate of divinity from his old university in 1689, and it is interesting to note that he was a foundation member of the Society for Promoting Christian Knowledge and one of the first incorporated members of the Society for the Propagation of the Gospel; he certainly played a very prominent part in the founding of these two great Church societies. He was a director of Greenwich Hospital and in 1707 was chosen president of Sion College. We are told that he continued to preach in his parish church until after his eightieth birthday; and before his retirement he put together a collection of his addresses and instructions in a volume entitled *The Principles and Duties of the Christian Religion*, a copy of which he presented to every householder in his parish. At his death he was, according to his wish, buried beneath the altar of the church that he had served for so long.

John Mapletoft was a true son of Little Gidding. In Ward's memoir we read that " he received the impressions of religion and virtue very early by the care of his great-uncle, Mr. Ferrar ".* We know that he inherited and cherished a number of family treasures, including the three volumes of the *Story Books* and the great Pentateuchal compilation which Prince Rupert had called " the gallantest, glorious, largest book " in the world. The first

* John Ward, *The Lives of the Professors of Gresham College* (London, 1740), p. 277.

volume of the *Story Books*, it may be remembered, was presented by Mary and Anna Collet to their sister Susanna, John Mapletoft's mother; and beneath the signatures of the " Maiden Sisters " John inscribed many years later the note:

" Who both died virgins, resolving so to live when they were young, by the grace of God.   My much honoured Aunt Mary, who took care of me and my brother Peter and Sister Mary after the death of our reverend and pious father, died in the 80th year of her age.

" John Mapletoft."

There is much in John Mapletoft's life and character that reminds us of Nicholas Ferrar.   Like Nicholas, he was a fine scholar, a master of the classics, well read in French, Spanish, and Italian. Both men had the gift of winning the affection of others and of holding the friendship of many different types of person.   The pattern of both their lives was entirely homogeneous, displaying a steady growth to spiritual manhood and marked by an unfailing serenity of mind and simplicity of heart.   Ward says of Mapletoft that " he was remarkable from his youth for sincere piety and devotion, which grew up with him into a settled habit, unaffected and free from all sourness and reserve ".

He was utterly negligent of fame or reputation; indeed, he carefully avoided such occasions and contacts as might have brought him into any prominence.   Many of his parishioners benefited by his generosity; he was constantly helping others and always lived very simply himself.   There was nothing of the easy-going Churchman about him.   He could speak with prophetic fire and he made stern demands on those who came to him for guidance.   We can see how strong and vigorous and un-compromising was his teaching if we turn to the pages of his *Principles and Duties of the Christian Religion*.   The book is arranged in twenty-six main sections and he explains in his preface how he wishes it to be used.   Much of the material, he says, will be familiar to his parishioners as having been delivered in sermons. But these plain statements of Christian truth need to be heard and heard again, and constantly considered and reflected upon.   His intention is that the book should be used for family reading on Sundays; one chapter may be taken each week or, by dividing the chapters, the reading may be spread over a year or longer. It is to be read aloud, normally by the head of the household; at the conclusion there should be a short silent period for reflection and prayer, and then questions should be asked and instruction given.   At the end of the book he provides a series of questions bearing on the subject-matter of each discourse. Finally, he includes a collection of prayers and collects for family use and a short and admirable account: " Of the Institution, Nature and End of the Lord's Supper and of the Preparation which is needful for the due Receiving it."

" For ", he says, " if men could once be prevailed upon duly to consider and to understand for themselves, without depending upon the bare affirmation of others, and to examine both themselves and others too under their care, how far they do understand these things, and then so to apply to themselves the great truths and duties of the Gospel as to be influenced and governed thereby, their lives would be more suitable to their profession, that is more Christian and more hopeful and more comfortable to their own selves; and their eternal welfare would be less hazardous (not to say hopeless) than it can be whilst they remain in such fatal ignorance and stupid neglect of what they are concerned above all things to consider and to know and to believe and to do." *

There can be few more excellent handbooks of sound, practical Christian teaching than the *Principles and Duties*.   It is clearly and simply written, wise and profound in counsel, learned without being in the least academic, urgent in its appeal.   It lacks the spiritual richness to be found in William Law; it is rather a guide to belief and conduct than to devotional practice, to the intent, as he tells his readers, that piety and universal holiness of heart and mind may be promoted, " giving us all good ground to hope for an happy and joyful meeting in the next world ".

* *The Principles and Duties of the Christian Religion*, etc., by John Mapletoft, D.D. (London, 1710), p. xvi.

There is a moderation and sobriety in his teaching that is characteristic of Anglican thought in Queen Anne's time. He was no extremist; his robust loyalty to the " good old way " of the church of his baptism was never in any way shaken. There was a good deal of interest in Little Gidding and its tradition amongst the Non-Jurors, but there is no suggestion that Mapletoft was ever drawn to the movement. The fact that he was a middle-aged man before he took orders may partly account for the fact that he stood aside from controversy; he was content to stay in his parish and look after his people.

" He led a long life ", says Ward, " with as much health of body and content of mind, in as much esteem and reputation of the world, and love and affection of his friends, as perhaps very few have done. His body decayed gently, but his mind not at all; and he was to the last as free from covetousness as ever, and ever preserved the cheerfulness and gaiety of his temper, and seemed desirous to gain the affection of those about him, that he might engage them to virtue and religion which he always inculcated upon them by good discourse, and books which he gave them and used to call his legacies."

And now, in conclusion, we may return to Little Gidding. In 1691, some ten years after Mary Collett's death, John Ferrar's grandson, the Reverend Thomas Ferrar, was instituted to the two rectorships of Steeple Gidding and Little Gidding. The former he was to retain for forty-eight years, until his death in 1739; the latter he resigned in 1707, when he became rector of Sawtry.

Born in 1663, Thomas Ferrar had been at Pembroke College, Cambridge, from 1679 till 1682. His long life was simply that of a dutiful country parson; he was a good scholar, he was assiduous in all his duties, and the glimpses that we have of him in his letters show him to have been a most kindly and lovable person. He was a man of omnivorous interests, perhaps one of those people who are constantly accumulating information about some particular subject with the obvious intention of writing about it, but who never, for one reason or another, find opportunity for assembling and composing their materials. It all remains in his note-books; before he has fully mastered whatever topic it may be, another of even more absorbing interest has suggested itself and he becomes engrossed in new provinces of research and discovery.   Amongst the voluminous papers in his handwriting in the Magdalene collection we find a series of bio-graphical notes about Cranmer; a chronology of world history; an annotated list of London churches destroyed in the Great Fire; an essay on methods of teaching English; a collection of epitaphs, some notes about coins, tables of the pedigrees of English ducal families, and lists of baptisms, marriages, and burials at Little Gidding.

There are a number of letters, all undated but probably written in the 1720's, to his son Jack, a Cambridge undergraduate.   They contain items of local and family news, instructions to the young man about sending his soiled linen home to be washed, an enquiry as to the opinion in Cambridge about the new state lotteries, corrections of his son's spelling mistakes, and so forth.

" I'm hard at work ", he writes on one occasion, " on Wells and Fuller's Geography, which are very improving and enter-taining.   But my desire looks like to be interrupted, for I am going to plough in Thorning field. . . . This place is very barren of news."

It seems clear that he planned to write something about his great-uncle, Nicholas Ferrar, for there are a series of biographical notes, some of which contain information that has survived in no other sources.   He must have known and used his grandfather's memoir of Nicholas, as well as other family papers; and it can be presumed that he was acquainted with the Reverend Francis Peck, whose life of Nicholas, under the title of *The Complete Church of England Man,* was finished shortly before the author's death in 1743, though, as we know, it was to be tragically lost half a century later.

Thomas Ferrar is an inconspicuous figure, but he should not be forgotten.   It was during his time that the restoration of Little Gidding church was carried out and the west front rebuilt as we see it to-day; we can be reasonably certain that he was actively concerned in this good work.   His brother John remained lord of the manor until 1748, when the estate passed finally out of the family.   Our last glimpse of Little Gidding comes from the Reverend Nicholas Brett, a non-juring clergyman who was for some years chaplain to the Cotton family.   Brett knew Little Gidding well and we have two letters of his to his father which describe the church as he saw it in 1743.   It had, he says, been rebuilt in brick and bonded upon the old stone pavement; the interior had been left unaltered.

" 'Tis wainscoted with good old oak and niches in the wainscoting for the congregation to sit in, quite without pews or benches in the middle.   Tis a very small building. . . . There are two handsome seats or rather thrones, much like the bishop's throne at Canterbury, but not so fine, on each side of the door, for the Master and Mistress, each facing the altar.   The pulpit and reading-desk are on each side of the door of the chancel; in short, the whole is very neat and pretty.   Just under the desk and pulpit is the Font, which is solid brass, and an eagle desk, also of brass, to answer to it; they are both so heavy that, when I try to lift them one by one, I cannot do it." *

Everything, in fact, remained much as it had been in Nicholas Ferrar's lifetime.   The manor-house was presumably still standing and we know nothing of the circumstances in which it was pulled down or of when this happened.   The house has now completely disappeared and even its site is not known with certainty.

Here, then, our narrative comes to its natural end.   A new chapter, marking the re-discovery of Little Gidding and the recognition of its place in the Anglican heritage, begins with the publication in 1793 of Peckard's memoir of Nicholas Ferrar and is continued through the nineteenth century with the appearance of further Little Gidding studies.   The moving account of the Ferrar household in Chapter IV of *John Inglesant*, published in 1881, enormously widened the interest of English Churchpeople in the story of Little Gidding;   several valuable books have appeared since that time and the bibliography of Little Gidding is now quite substantial.   That the story makes both an appeal

---

* H. P. K. Skipton, " Little Gidding and the Non-Jurors ", *Church Quarterly Review*, October 1921.

and a challenge to the present day is shown in many ways, notably, perhaps, in the large number of pilgrimages made to Little Gidding and in the recognition that it is still, and will always remain, a hallowed place, rendered so by the lives of that " congregation of saints " three hundred years ago.

INDEX